I am a Runner

The Memoirs of a Sepsis Survivor

Maria Papalia-Meier
with
Pamela Ackerson

Push past the wall
Pamela Ackerson

I am a Runner

The Memoirs of a Sepsis Survivor

Maria Papalia-Meier
and
Pamela Ackerson

©Maria Papalia-Meier 2019

All rights reserved.
No part of this book may be reproduced or utilized in any form by any means, electronic or mechanical, including photocopying or recording, or by any information storage and retrieval system, without permission in writing from the publisher.

Cover Design: Dora Gonzalez (PremadeCovers4U.com)
Rachel M. Christian
Editing: Stephanie Taylor

Disclaimer:

I am a Runner – The Memoirs of a Sepsis Survivor is an account of the real events of Maria Papalia-Meier. Due to a short period of time when she was comatose, events which weren't recalled by Ms. Papalia-Meier were drawn from a variety of sources, interviews, and memories of close friends and family. There are no dramatic or fictional scenes, dialogues, or composites. Names have been changed to protect the privacy of the individuals.

"I have my own unique road that has had many exciting ups and heart-breaking downs, but one thing I know is that my journey is not over and the best is yet to come." ~ Ryan Hall

US Olympic Marathoner, and founder of Steps Foundation
Author of **Run the Mile You're In**
RyanandSaraHall.com

Dedication:

I would like to thank the following people who kept me sane, helped keep me positive, and striving toward my ultimate goals, those who prayed for me and my family, and stood by us during a most tragic moment of our lives.

My husband, Myatt
My son, Carson
My daughter, Emma
My mother, Sandy
My brother, Johnny
My sister, Michelle

    To all of our family, friends, and neighbors, you have been a huge blessing: The doctors and nurses of the Brigham, Norwood, and Dedham medical centers and hospitals. The paramedics and EMTs in the ambulances who took me to the hospitals and rehab facility. The Plainville People, OOFOS and their employees.

    Everyone took time away from something else they could've been doing and helped us. I've appreciated your prayers, positive vibes, and heartfelt texts.

    I must also thank the countless unknown people who came in and out of my rooms when I was unconscious. Those unsung guardians need a special thanks of appreciation.

    God was with us. With Him, and all of you, I have nothing to fear.

List of Medical Abbreviations:

AC — Artificial corporeal life support and Assist Control
Amiodarone — A medication affecting the heartbeat, and is used to keep a normal rhythm for people with life-threatening heart rhythm disorders.
ARDS — Acute respiratory distress syndrome caused by inflammation of the lungs.
CAT or CT scan — A computerized axial tomography or a computerized tomography is an imaging procedure using special x-ray equipment. It scans an area inside the body.
CCs — Cubic Centimeters, a metric measurement for fluids.
CO2 — Carbon dioxide
CVVH — Continuous veno-venous hemofiltration is a treatment used on patients with acute or chronic renal failure.
ECMO — Extra-corporeal membrane oxygenation (ECMO), also known as extracorporeal life support (ECLS). A medical technique used to provide prolonged cardiac and respiratory support when the heart and lungs are unable to sustain life.
EKG — An electrocardiogram that records the electrical activity of the heart. Also known as an ECG
LVEF — A left ventricular ejection fraction is the percentage of the blood pumped out of the heart's main pumping chamber during a contraction.
MRI — A magnetic resonance imaging test that takes detailed pictures of the inside of the body using powerful magnets and radio waves.
MRSA — Methicillin-resistant staphylococcus aureus is a bacteria causing infection. It's resistant to commonly used

antibiotics, making it difficult to treat than most staph infections.

Pressor — A chemical substance used to raise blood pressure.

PFC — Perfluorocarbons (use of liquid ventilation)

PSV — Pressure support ventilation

ST myocardial infarction — term used by cardiologist to describe a typical heart attack.

Trach — A breathing tube place through a hole into the windpipe to assist breathing.

TTE — A transthoracic echocardiogram checks the heart and blood vessels near the heart for any problems.

Introduction
Chapter One
Chapter Two
Chapter Three
Chapter Four
Chapter Five
Chapter Six
Chapter Seven
Chapter Eight
Chapter Nine
Chapter Ten
Chapter Eleven
Chapter Twelve
Documentation and Letters
Images
Warning some images may cause discomfort.
Informational Links

Maria Papalia-Meier

June 18, 2014 @ 9:28 pm

"I had no idea how much I loved my wife until today. She is the best thing that has ever happened to me.

I love you, Maria Papalia-Meier."

Introduction

The world was perfect.

Yes, I know. Nothing is perfect. Let me rephrase it for the pessimists.

My world was perfect. Even with the typical ups and downs of life, it was a good life. I was healthy. I exercised. I ran almost every day. I had an awesome husband, great kids, the best of friends, and a kick-butt career.

What could possibly go wrong?

Those people who think *half-empty* would disagree with me. They'd have the attitude of 'just wait' something will go wrong.

Well, it did. My world had its own personal apocalypse.

From a bird's eye view, I was the person standing in the middle of the road surrounded by complete and utter destruction.

But I wasn't going to allow it to hold me down.

Why?

Because I'm a fighter, and I refused to let it break me.

I had my faith.

I had my family.

And I had my husband.

And with all of this combined, I could do anything.

And that *anything* was to survive near death caused by sepsis and multiple complications.

From the ashes...I became a runner.

My name is Maria Papalia-Meier. On June 18, 2014, my life changed. I went septic from a strep infection. I was unaware of how sick I was, nor how close I came to death.

I want to give you a little insight into who I am and the deep-seated influences from friends, family, and parents.

My best friend Joanna has been with me through thick and thin. She moved into our neighborhood when she was three. Her mom, along with Joanna, came to our door and introduced themselves.

We spent a lot of time together and were included in each other's family vacations.

She was embarrassed at times by some of her father's sense of humor and antics. I personally found them entertaining. As best friends do, we hung out together doing our hair, playing music, swimming, and other normal kid things.

My dad was a great man. He was considerably older than my mother. With thirty years between them, he used to joke around about how he grew up with my friends' grandparents instead of their parents.

Our house was the place where the neighborhood kids wanted to play. He used to love playing baseball with us. Since he couldn't run, he was crowned the all-time pitcher.

He owned his own business and my mother worked with him as his secretary. He had Parkinson's disease, and as it progressed, my mother tended to his increasing needs.

When I was in high school, he went into a hospital in New York for surgery on his spine. I was distraught and didn't want him to leave. He reassured me it would be a good thing. He'd be able to walk without a cane.

He was there for a month. My mother flew to New York sometimes staying for days and other times flying back the same day.

She didn't like being away from him.

In many ways, I see myself in her. I'm not in high spirits when I'm away from my husband, Myatt, either. We have a special love that is hard to find. We're lucky. Not everyone can find this kind of love and devotion in a marriage.

My dad was a good listener; and was always there for me. He paid attention to detail and was never judgmental. He was respectful and was chock-full of integrity.

He had so much joy and happiness in him, and he wanted to make sure we did, too. Birthdays and Christmas' were his favorite times. He loved buying us presents.

I recall one year when I wanted a kitten. My mother said no. We came home with two. That way the kitty wouldn't be lonely, and they had a friend.

Years later, while living in Atlanta, I got the dreaded call. *Come home.*

Things weren't looking good. Grabbing the first flight available, I prayed the whole time I'd get there before it was too late.

To see him one more time and to hear his beautiful voice would hold me for the rest of my life. I was able to say my goodbye and spend time with him before he passed.

Mom was there with him the whole time, and it was wearing on her. We sent her home. She was getting sick and was suffering from exhaustion.

Those last moments with him was a gift I'll always cherish.

He passed away in 1999.

My mom, AKA Sandy.

I don't call my mom, Sandy, out of disrespect or because she's my stepmother. When we were younger, she said she was tired of hearing Mom, Mom, Mom, all the time. So I started calling her Sandy.

My mother, like most awesome mothers, doesn't get enough credit for all the things she has done. For years, she held our family together. She helped run the family business, raised three children, and worked for the school district.

Even when my father was bed-ridden, she worked full time. Then, came home to take care of three kids, and my father.

As a working mother, I have a better understanding of how hard it was for each of them. It was hard for my father, who'd always been self-sufficient and independent. To have to depend on someone to help with the simplest things had to have been tough and humbling.

Yes, ironic, isn't it? To find myself in the exact same situation...

I also understand how frustrating it was for my mother to constantly have to care for those around her. It was tiring to work a full day, come home, cook, clean, take care of three kids, and an invalid husband.

A part of my mother died with him. As far as I know, she hasn't gotten into a relationship since my father passed away.

She misses him every day.

Seriously, I'm surprised she hadn't ripped her hair out in frustration. I completely get it. I understand why she was a little short-tempered.

Not only was she my father's caretaker, she helped with his sisters as well. She's a nurturing, loving caretaker. She's made a lot of sacrifices for her family.

With her always being there for me, it'll be nice to have someone pamper and take care of her for once.

Mom is one strong woman. I can't imagine how hard it was for her.

One thing comes to mind. I always wanted my mother when I was under the weather, no matter how old I was. I remember freaking out my college roommate, Mikki, when I was sick. I was on the top bunk and began banging on the wall, yelling for my mother.

Mikki was like a sister to me. We went to high school together and our first two years of community college. I started calling her Mikki because she shares my sister's name and it became easier with the nickname.

I managed to convince her to move south with me. Once I was accepted to Georgia Southern University, she decided to go tour the school. Her dad fell in love with the campus and teased her. If she didn't go to the university, he would.

She took care of me when I needed her most.

My parents' bedroom was next to mine. When I was sick, I banged on the wall so she came in and took care of me.

Even now, as an adult, I still call her to let her know. Somehow, her advice always gives comfort and reassurance.

I always said I wouldn't get married until I found someone who looked at me and loved me as much as my parents loved each other.

My husband, Myatt, and I met in Atlanta. He was hired as a Special Assignment Manager for the company where I worked.

Since I've always been sociable, especially to new friends and acquaintances who didn't know anyone, I included him in many of our gatherings. I enjoy helping people, and making them welcome.

My husband calls me a community organizer.

Even though Myatt and I were getting to know each other better, I wasn't looking for a relationship.

We hit it off right from the start. He was charming and funny, and his humor was one of his most endearing qualities.

He tells people he married me because he was going bald and had to settle.

One night while eating wings at a casual restaurant in Atlanta, Myatt said, "Either we start dating or just be friends. But we have to make it official."

Completely out of character for me, we ended up moving in together six month after we started dating.

I was telling him my roommate, without consulting me, asked her boyfriend to move in with us. To make matters worse, he wasn't going to be splitting the rent.

I wasn't happy. Myatt suggested I move in with him. He had a two-bedroom apartment and had room for a roommate. After I moved in, we sat down to figure out a budget. I needed to contribute although he never made me pay rent.

On one of our evenings out, we were discussing a budget and decided to merge our money together.

He said, "It doesn't matter. We're going to get married anyway."

My heart was full. I finally met my soulmate.

Myatt became a consultant with another company. It was a great job and allowed us to travel.

Coming home alone from our honeymoon was a forlorn, deflating emotion.

He had to return to D.C.

It was a slight snare from our jovial world. We returned from our glorious honeymoon and our friend met us at the airport to pick me up. I gave Myatt a quick kiss in baggage claim with his suitcase full of clothes for the week.

After such an emotional high from our wedding; and the fun we had during the week, walking into our home alone as a new bride was unnerving. It was upsetting. My happiness and elation fizzled faster than a balloon popping.

Each week, I went with Myatt to the airport on Sundays, and picked him up on Fridays.

I didn't like being without him. I'm still that way.

With his traveling, our time was limited. I avoided arguing with him. After my father passed away, I had a hard time saying goodbye. I was always worried it would be our last.

But our happily-ever-after continued. We were moving furniture around the house, and I started craving ice cream. I wanted a hot fudge sundae. That's when it hit me. I was slightly grumpy, and hadn't had my cycle in a while.

I giggled. "Maybe I should take a pregnancy test."

I took the test, and we continued to move furniture.

It was positive.

I said. "We didn't get the answer we were looking for."

Myatt grinned from ear to ear. It was the answer he was looking for.

I was pregnant.

What were we going to do with a baby? Myatt traveled for work. I traveled for my job. We didn't have any family close to us to help.

The pregnancy prompted him to get off the road. He wanted to be around as a full-time father, not only for weekends. He knew someone who worked as a district manager for a large retail pharmacy. Myatt arranged an interview, and was hired. He started working as a store manager. He did what needed to be done for his family.

Life was good. I had a C-section, and we welcomed a beautiful baby boy.

When my son was born, my brother asked if I was going to quit work and stay home. I didn't see the need. I was comfortable with using daycare.

I believed they needed me more once they hit school age. I'd be there when they arrived home from school, and I could join them with their extracurricular activities.

If they had a hard day, we could talk about it.

Myatt tends to see the potential in different situations. He wanted more. More for himself, and more for our family. It was a good position. But it wasn't his dream job.

In 2006, we were ready to add another little bundle of joy to our family. Staying at a hotel in Birmingham, I kept sneezing and my eyes itched from the feather pillows.

It was unusual, and obviously, something was up. I took the pregnancy test when I got home.

Myatt had an opportunity for a promotion. Nevertheless, if he wanted the position, he'd have to transfer. It was in the New England area.

Being the salesman he was, he attempted to sell it to me. "You'll be closer to your mom, sister, and brother."

I wanted to be the good wife, and encouraged him. It gnawed at me. I had no desire to leave Georgia and relocate. We lived north of Atlanta in a cute little neighborhood at the top of the cul-de-sac. I was fortunate.

I didn't want to leave.

I didn't think he'd be offered the position. Not because he wasn't qualified or perfect for the job, but because there'd be a lot of people wanting the position who lived closer and were qualified.

Well, I was wrong. Myatt was offered the position.

It didn't go over well. "I'm grateful you were offered the job. Congratulations, but I'm not moving."

The discussions went back and forth and eventually he declined the offer, explaining the cost-of-living, his wife would need to find a job, etc.

They wanted him, and were willing to compensate us. In the end, it was too good to pass up.

While I was in the hospital to have the baby via C-section, Myatt told me the *for-sale* sign was up.

I cried. I loved my house.

Emma was born on July 19, 2007.

After she was born, I started running again. It was relaxing. It was a great way to exercise and kept me emotionally balanced and focused.

Myatt traveled back and forth to Rhode Island until the house was sold, and we were able to join him. The plan was to hand in my notice when I returned from maternity leave.

It wasn't easy dealing with a long distance relationship. There weren't any openings available for a transfer, and we couldn't live on one salary.

I didn't move to New England until two years after Myatt took the position. We finally managed to move to New England in 2009, right before Christmas.

We were miserable.

I didn't want to be there. With Myatt traveling back and forth to Puerto Rico, it certainly didn't help things during the transition. The children and I fended for ourselves.

We weren't used to the cold or snow. It was a culture shock. We didn't need four-wheel drive vehicles in Georgia. I was terrified driving in the snow, sleet, finding black ice… I recall one occasion I was gripping the steering wheel so tight, it hurt my fingers. My heart was racing and my breathing was so erratic, I was lightheaded. It was so severe. I swear my blood wasn't reaching my brain. I parked the car on the side of the road and planned on walking the rest of the way home.

I may have grown up in upstate New York, but it was more than ten years since I drove in freezing, snowy weather.

I thought I was going to implode when Myatt had the audacity to send me a delightful picture of a sunny beach from Puerto Rico.
Thanks, buddy.

It was hard leaving my job, neighbors, and friends. They became family.

Once I started back to work, the children were at a daycare. When they started school, it was necessary to change things to a more positive home atmosphere.

They did an after-school program for a bit, but we felt they were missing out on real neighborhood camaraderie and fun. The children would be happier coming home from school instead of participating in the after-school program.

Finding a home caretaker for the children was a priority.

We met Celeste through a website which recommended babysitters and caretakers.

We decided a sitter would come to the house and watch the kids after school until we got home from work.

It was obvious we were unprepared for her interview. We hadn't used a sitter before and had no clue what to do, what to ask, or what to expect.

Common sense had us ask for references, experience, etc., but anything else was beyond us. Our children were no longer babies. If there was a problem, or they didn't like her, they'd say something.

Celeste was in high school when she started watching the children for us. She was wonderful. Not only did the kids like her, but she was the favorite in the neighborhood as well.

She was fun and entertained them. She played with both of them, helped with homework, played sports, did crafts, and interacted with them.

Sometimes, the children would ask if they could stay up later, or do something, and we'd tell them to ask Celeste.

She was in charge.

We trusted her.

The most precious thing Celeste did for my children was be there for them while I was hospitalized and recuperating.

She was there during the most difficult part of their lives. She was a stronghold for them.

She got them through it.

Even after I came home, she was there for us. I couldn't drive, and had a hard time taking care of myself. She picked up the slack. She became the loving mother's helper, doing everything I did before my dreadful battle with sepsis.

We trusted her that much.

It didn't stop at driving the children to the extracurricular activities and babysitting, she lent a hand with me as well. If I needed anything from the store, or needed to go somewhere, she was willing to help.

We were lucky and knew it. We were surrounded by loving people. Celeste was a rare gem. She handled the situation with maturity, responsibility, and elegance.

She will forever be a part of our family.

New Year 2014, my close friend, Allie, came to visit. It made the transition slightly easier. Although, I cried when she left. Her family came to visit the New Year's before I was admitted to the hospital, stayed for a few days, and headed to Vermont for some skiing fun.

It was odd. Before she left, I grew nervous.

I was scheduled to have a hysterectomy in February. I took the BRCA test and had a positive result for being prone to breast and/or ovarian cancer.

At the time, the best prevention was a hysterectomy and I agreed to the surgery.

I told her it might be the last time I saw her. I was antsy about the operation, and had an overwhelming feeling of impending disaster. My racing heart indicated the anxiety pumping through my brain.

I didn't intentionally want to make her uncomfortable. I truly believed it'd be the last time I would see her.

After we moved to New England, I found it hard to run. It was arctic bone-chilling weather, and the motivation escaped me. Not being able to run made me miserable.

I am a Runner

It didn't last. When there's a problem, I fixed it. I began running with a neighbor. After a while, we formed a neighborhood group. We ran 5Ks together and planned on continuing to run longer and do half-marathons.

I'll be honest. I didn't want to move. I made it down-right, out-right arduous for Myatt. As bad as I made it for him, he still didn't want to call it quits.

I had myself a keeper.

Knowing how hard I fought the move to New England, it was ironic how it ended up being a decision which saved my life.

Chapter One

Why do I run?

I was living in Savannah, GA working my first job at a staffing service, and I was on again off again with a guy I dated through high school and college. I was having pains which, I assumed, was gas. It got so bad I couldn't lie down, get in the car, or move about without hurting.

My boss, Becca said if I didn't make a doctor's appointment she'd make one for me. I was terrified. My imagination escalated from gas to cancer. I was certain I wasn't going to make it.

The doctor's examination resulted in a diagnosis of IBS, irritable bowel syndrome. According to him, type A personalities are prone to the syndrome. He suggested I run or jog to relieve tension.

I'm not the type of person who can let go of difficulties and stress. I'm a borderline perfectionist. I needed to be in control of my life, and little tribulations got in my way of happiness.

It's impossible to be able to control every aspect of our lives. But I sure did try. And it definitely stressed me out.

I wanted to be the perfect person, the one our friends talked to, went to help for, cried to, and wanted to have fun with, etc. I wanted to be the best, and I compelled myself to be an overachiever.

The need to be the best added to my insecurities about not being good enough, and caused more angst in my life than necessary.

Running was a good suggestion. It helped relieve my tension and worries.

It'd been a while since I ran, so I needed to start slow. A woman I worked with offered to run with me. We ran a few miles during our lunch hour and went to the lake close to where we worked. Daily runs became a part of my routine.

Life continued, and I started dating a gentleman who ran with me. We ran at the lake after work. During the holidays, we ran at Forsyth Park. It was beautiful at Christmas time.

I had a runner's high. I looked forward to it every day. I especially liked running in the heat, 85° to 90° was perfect!

I remember one of my first 5Ks was during Oktoberfest in Savannah. My friend's husband was the director of the YMCA, and he was in charge of the race. Darlene and I raced together for years.

After moving to Atlanta, I continued to run in the race in Savannah. It became a tradition. The best thing of all was the cold beer waiting at the end! It sure beat a banana... especially in the heat.

We had a great group of friends.

I met Allie Edgar and her husband while living in an apartment complex in Atlanta. One year we got tickets to Steeplechase, and we had a table up front.

Steeplechase is a gathering of equestrian enthusiasts who come together to help several Georgia charities. It's a sensational southern tradition.

Not knowing what was expected, Allie helped us with the social requirements. It was a wonderful time. We were invited to a private party and danced for hours.

Someone snapped our picture and we made the front page of the small town paper!

When they moved from Atlanta, I was devastated.

Whenever they came back to town, Allie made sure they would visit.

One time, she was in Auburn for the Ole Miss Vs Auburn game and decided to come and visit. She brought the kids with her and went trick or treating with us.

I started working for FedEx, and continued to run until my job consumed most of my time. My schedule was full. I was in a grad school program. Between classes and work, running was put on the back burner.

I wanted to lose the last little bit of baby weight I gained, and started again after my first child. I joined a group at our local YMCA.

It was managed by a woman named Renee. I will never forget her. She went through her own personal ordeal, and found it as a useful way to help. It didn't only help with weight loss but as a positive and healthy mood-lifter. Until I was stronger and able to keep up with the group, she ran at my pace.

I really enjoyed our runs. We ran on the weekends, meeting at the Marietta Square. The square was a pretty area with shops and restaurants. We rewarded ourselves with a cup of coffee and a little something sweet at the Australian deli.

My endurance increased, and we moved our runs to Kennesaw Mountain. I stopped at the Starbucks on my way home for coffee and banana bread.

When Myatt began working in Rhode Island, he was motivated to get into shape. We worked out a goal, and planned to run our first 5K together on St. Patrick's Day.

St. Patrick's Day arrived. It was a miserable 40°, and raining. I was slouching on the couch wishing he'd want to cancel. Nope, not Myatt. He enthusiastically bounced down the steps, calling out. "Let's go!"

We had the best time. He understood why I loved to run and why I enjoyed the 5Ks. We stuck to our schedule and did one a month.

The races were early in the morning. After the races, we'd have breakfast and make it home with plenty of time to spend time with the kids.

It feels good when I run. I'm happier, and I get a lot done. Running in the morning, when most people aren't awake yet, is especially peaceful for me.

When I run without a companion, I don't listen to music. I enjoy my surroundings. I love listening to nature's songs, and absorbing the beauty around me. It's my time.

I relish the fresh air, and release the aggravations and pressures clouding my happiness. Each step is a tread away from the flooding static filtering its way into our lives. The constant pinging is unsettling and running kept it at an acceptable balance.

There's an inner peace and stillness within me. It was, and is, calming. It's my personal way of meditating.

I avoid thinking about the million little things. I seize the excessive thinking and clear my mind. I would get to the obligations of the day, and the crucial business I had to do when I finished my run.

Once in a while, I catch myself thinking about difficulties or issues, but I shimmy those thoughts over and concentrate on the beauty around me.

I'm amazed at how I see something different each time. Even though my route's the same. It's the simple things; how pretty someone's garden looks, the way they decorated their front porch, or the beautiful trees in someone's yard.

When I run with a companion, we usually talk. Mom-chatter about kids, vacation adventures, or the funny things that happened during the week.

Our first winter in New England, I tried to run. We moved north in December. The winter's a lot different here than in Atlanta. Living in the south, I ran during my lunch break, the park was about a mile down the road. I dressed in long-johns, a heavy coat, gloves, and hat. Most southern winter days were around 50°. You know, *Georgia* cold.

Running during the New England winters made me miserable. The bone chilling, jaw-clenching shivers pushed the misery in the forefront. I was over it.

I would turn around, go home, put on jogging pants, and bundle up on the couch. It was so much better. The warmth of the house was a huge, comforting hug.

I went to the gym on and off, but it wasn't consistent.

At the time, my husband wasn't able to run with me. Since Emma was little, I decided to buy a bicycle. I rode with her in the back. It was okay.

By the end of the winter, I started meeting the neighbors. Leigh Ann wanted to run and having a companion was a good thing at the time.

Leigh Ann lived next door with her husband and two girls. When we moved into the house, Emma became friends with her daughter.

I was motivated to lose some of the weight. It was the perfect way for me to de-stress.

It was pretty much experiencing cabin fever. I was grumpy most of the time, tired, and not myself.

Leigh Ann and I ran every day before I went to work. Five a.m. was our usual start time. I was able run and catch the ferry to Nantucket or Martha's Vineyard to be to work on time.

I couldn't believe I was doing this at five o'clock in the morning with temperatures occasionally dipping below zero. I think I lost my mind. How crazy was I to be voluntarily out in below zero weather?

Nevertheless, I realized I found my sanity. I felt good when I ran, and it quenched and satisfied my soul.

Leigh Ann and I became friends as well as running partners. We added a few more to our group. We ran a few 5Ks together. But as things happen, our small group gradually dwindled down again.

It was only us diehards now: me, Leigh Ann, and our other neighbor, Vicki. We decided to sign up for our first half marathon.

We had our run on the Monday before I was admitted into the hospital.

I was training for this when I first got sick. We ran six to eight miles on the weekend, three during the week, and averaged about twenty-eight miles a week.

Chapter Two

Boston is known for having the best medical facilities in the world. All too soon, I found out how much I needed them.

It was too easy to ignore the symptoms. Most were typical. If I had prior knowledge or experience, I'd have known there'd be a need for concern.

I rationalized what was happening, setting aside the signs as normal for someone getting ill.

The fever told me I was getting the flu.

The rash, poison ivy I thought I'd gotten into while I was working in the yard.

Darkened urine, I was dehydrated because I was sick.

Tired and weak, bed-rest was needed since I had the flu.

I decided to take a couple pain relievers and go to work. There was too much to do to stay home bedridden.

I went to work at one of my stations on Monday, and set up my computer. I don't know what happened, but I didn't feel right.

I wasn't *me*.

There were a lot of things I needed to get done and then I would leave. I texted my husband to say I was going home because I was under the weather.

I honestly don't remember how I got home, but when I did, I went right to bed. I was shivering and moaning.

Monday night I asked Myatt for ginger ale, water, tea, and crackers. We both believed I had the flu, and I asked Myatt if he thought I was going to die…like always when I wasn't well.

I remember telling him to sleep on the couch so he wouldn't get sick.

Tuesday morning I decided I was in no condition to go to work. I received a few calls on my work cell phone and answered a few.

I remember saying I was unwell, and telling them to speak with someone else. It was out of character for me.

I stayed in bed, in pain and moaning because I couldn't get comfortable. I decided to take a warm shower.

My legs were stiff. My body shook as I leaned onto the tile wall. I could barely stand. I had piteous visions of paramedics rescuing me as I lay naked in the shower. I managed to sit on the little ledge.

Myatt was at work, but I cried for him, thinking how much having the flu sucked.

When he arrived home, I told him how terrible I was feeling and whimpered about how I was dying. I called the doctor, and he recommended a visit if there wasn't any improvement.

A good night's rest would help.

The symptoms started getting worse. Myatt came home early from work, and we went to the doctor. I was in severe pain and extremely weak. I had a hard time walking and needed to rest a few times before making it to the doctor's office.

I was slightly feverish, and my head was throbbing. My throat burned, and my muscles and bones ached. They were screaming at me. Of course, all of this was topped with exhaustion.

I was groaning and was short of breath. I could tell by the look on his face he thought I was exaggerating. I understand his attitude.

Prior behavior on my part for many years was to embellish my illnesses. I hated being sick, so I was always 'dying'. So when I moaned, he took it as typical me dramatizing my illness.

Myatt helped me walk to the office. My legs were laden with unseen lead, my head felt like a vice was clasped to my temples, and I attempted to sit in the elevator. I was deteriorating with each assisted step, shaking and feeble with each pain-wracking movement.

I remember laying my head on Myatt's lap. I think that's when he knew I was really out of sorts. They took me to a room right away so I could lie down while I was waiting for the doctor.

I figured I was dehydrated. The doctor would hook up an IV and be sent home.

I placed an aberrant effect on my positive attitude. It created an imagined phobia causing anxiety and trepidation. My imagination took over, and I was in trouble.

Unfortunately, this time I wasn't aggrandizing the pain and discomfort.

I have a fear of dying. I don't want to leave my kids, my family, nor my husband. I certainly, as selfish as it sounds, didn't want him finding someone else to love. My insecurities would creep out from their negative abyss, and I would have heart-wrenching nightmares he'd find a woman nicer than me, who treated him better, and then he'd forget about me, and all the magnificent times we had together.

A statistician will tell you dying is a numbers game. They throw percentages out there for us to see with every medicine commercial and doctor's evaluation.

It couldn't be *my* number hitting the reaper's roulette table.

We had no clue I really was on the brink of death.

They took my temperature and did a strep test.

They had trouble getting my blood pressure.

The doctor ordered an oxygen mask and an ambulance was called.

Things got a bit foggy from there.

I asked the ambulance paramedic, "Am I going to die? Please don't let me die."

My last memories were being rolled into the ambulance.

Maria Papalia-Meier

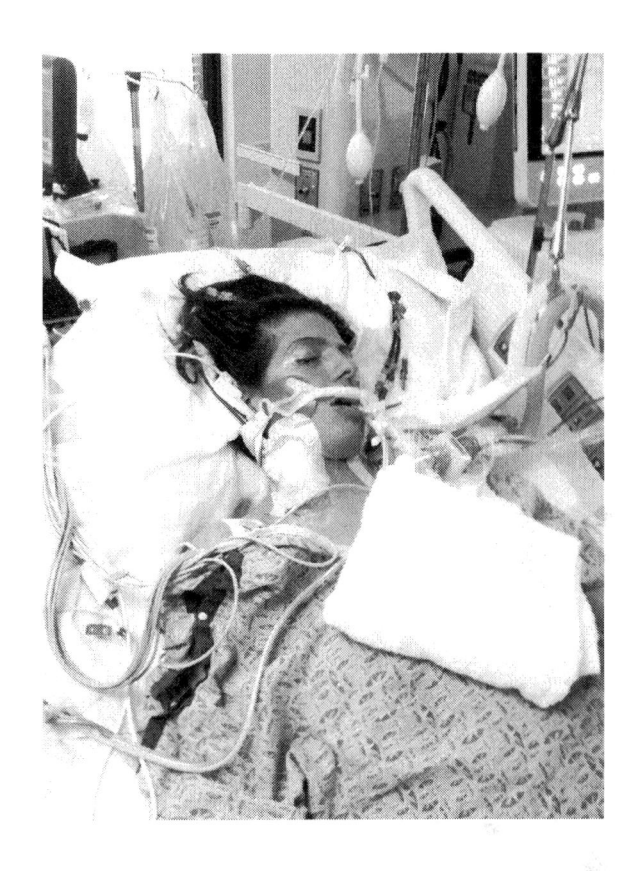

Myatt (Filling in the Missing Pieces of Memory)

Maria was hooked up to an IV and machines. The staff needed to evaluate and measure the oxygen content in her blood. Her blood pressure was so low they were having a hard time reading it. There were several things they needed to do and asked me to leave the room.

The doctor came to the waiting area. They believed she had pneumonia. I needed to sign a consent form to intubate her, to put a tube in to help her breathe. When I asked the doctor if Maria would be okay, he was uncertain, and said they'd do what they could.

They'd be taking her to ICU.

I went down the hall and found a secluded area. I lost it. The woman who was my life, and my love, might not make it out of the hospital alive.

Once I pulled myself together, I took a deep breath. I called her mother, sister, and brother.

I called Celeste to see if she could stay at the house until I got home. She stayed with them the first night and was there whenever our family couldn't be there.

Maria was heavily sedated. She tried talking to me, and attempted to write a note on my hand. The nurse said she'd never seen anything like it.

The strep had gotten into her bloodstream. The nurses and doctors were doing everything they possibly could.

I tried to comfort her and keep her calm. I imagine her sedation was a big help. I made every effort to stay positive in front of her.

I don't mind admitting; I cried like a baby in the waiting room.

I thought about all the great times we had together, the kids, our trip to Aruba, and the laughter.

We did a lot of laughing.

My heart broke when I faced reality. I might have to tell the kids the doctors couldn't save her.

I deliberated about what a wonderful mom she was. I realized how much she did. I hadn't appreciated all the work she did. She was the primary care-giver. Maria took care of them, from school to getting them to their activities, making sure they ate healthy, exercised, and be good honest people, etc.

It was horrible to think of losing her. Had I shown Maria how much I appreciated her, the way I should have? Did I show her how much I loved her?

I love you, Maria. One hundred times, I love you.

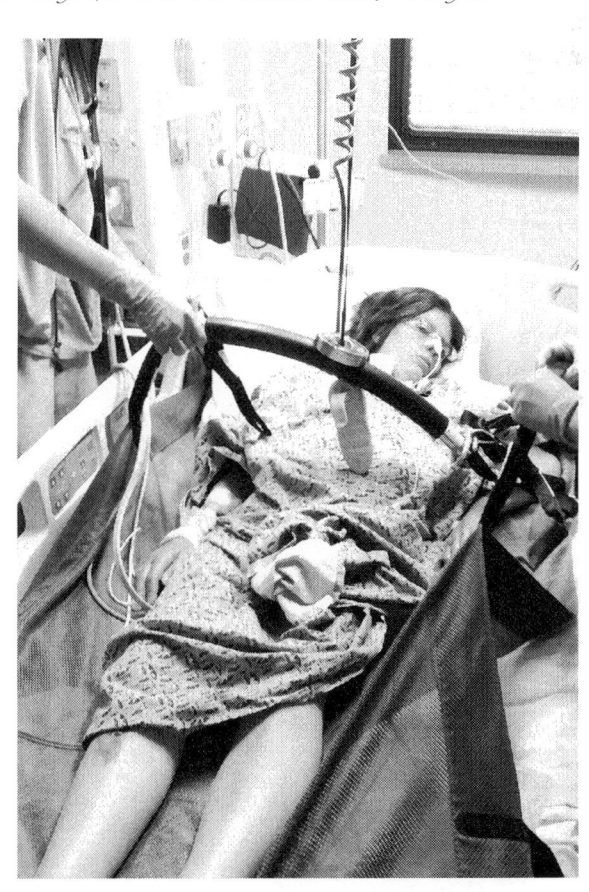

I told her brother, Johnny, and sister, Michelle, and her mother they needed to get here. I didn't tell them what the doctor said. I didn't want them to panic.

I spoke to a couple of friends, Russell and Nancee, who were in the medical field. I heard the Red Sox game in the background. I vividly recall his words and heard concern in his voice.

"If you're asking me if this was Nancee, I'd transfer her to Brigham's Woman's Hospital. Yes, I think Maria needs to be somewhere else."

Later in the evening, I started texting Russell. He was asleep and Nancee answered the texts. I asked about the process of getting Maria transferred to Brigham and who I needed to contact to do it.

Nancee texted a friend who worked in the towers and asked for advice. She didn't have much to offer. She made a point to say I had the right to get Maria transferred and needed to be persistent. She gave information on how to request a transfer, and how to get it expedited properly.

I followed their advice.

The doctor tended to Maria on a closed circuit TV and was directing the nurse. It wasn't a comforting situation. I called Maria's uncle and asked if he could stay on the phone in case I forgot to ask anything.

I asked the doctor, "Is she stable?"

"You mean stable enough to be transported?"

I answered, "Yes. I couldn't live with myself knowing one of the best hospitals in the country is only sixteen miles away."

Maria's uncle had me ask, "On a scale of one to ten, how sick is she?"

The doctor responded, "Approaching ten."

The doctor didn't disagree and filed the transfer request. The nurse reassured me I made the right decision.

The transport team arrived and were awesome. They were confident and reassuring. She was settled and ready for the ambulatory transport.

I completely believed if we got Maria to Brigham, she'd be okay.

The Norwood emergency doctor asked to speak with me. He believed transporting her was dangerous. He also said she'd need dialysis, and they couldn't perform dialysis at Norwood.

We were pretty much damned if we do, and damned if we didn't. I was beginning to second-guess my instincts and intuition.

The transport team overheard the conversation. They transported patients who were in worse shape than Maria, and didn't understand his concerns.

I wasn't sure if it was true, or if they were merely trying to reassure me. It didn't matter. It was what I needed to hear.

It made me feel better.

Johnny and I drove together to Brigham Hospital and arrived before the transport.

The transfer process to Brigham took about six hours from the time I asked to the time she arrived at 1:15 Thursday morning.

We couldn't see her right away, but the doctors gave us an explanation of what happened.

The strep infection entered Maria's bloodstream and turned into bacteria. The bacteria put an acid in her bloodstream and caused her veins and arteries to dilate.

The dilation created an issue with her blood pressure. It dropped because there wasn't enough blood volume to keep the pressure up.

The trickle of disaster continued when her heart rate increased and compensated for the lack of blood volume.

Both medical facilities gave her fluids to treat the issues. The fluids helped fill her circulatory system, which in turn, would raise her blood pressure.

Due to the infection plowing through her veins, arteries, and capillaries, she was unable to hold the fluid and it began to seep into her tissue.

At nineteen liters of fluid, they reached a point where they couldn't give her any more.

They began using pressors, a chemical agent for raising blood pressure.

They used it to constrict the blood flow to her extremities in order for it to flow to her vital organs and sustain blood pressure.

It did its job.

Unfortunately, the pressor can reduce and restrict blood flow to the extremities, and it caused necrosis to occur in her hands, fingers, and toes.

They had her on a ventilator for oxygen, but her lungs were filled with fluids. It wasn't operating well enough to remove CO2 from her blood and oxygen.

Overall, she was in horrible shape.

The doctor mentioned a potential option called ECMO. They needed to review Maria's case. She wasn't an ideal candidate. It was usually reserved for patients who had heart and lung transplants.

I pleaded with him and asked to speak to the team of doctors. I explained Maria was young, and healthy, with small kids. I was practically begging. I couldn't take care of them without her. He agreed to speak to the team.

And then, we waited.

A few hours later, the ECMO team arrived. The doctors spoke about the risks of having her on the machine. I signed for the treatment.

At the time, I didn't realize the doctors considered it a last resort to keep her alive.

One of the doctors returned, informing me they requested a surgical consult. Because of the different risks, I wasn't sure if she'd be put on the ECMO.

When the doctor said Maria went into cardiac arrest, I thought the procedure and life support was out of the question at this point.

I was petrified.

The doctors informed me they'd be doing the procedure for ECMO.

Once the ECMO was turned on, the oxygen level in her blood went into the nineties. For the moment, one issue was resolved.

They continued to add the pressors to keep her blood pressure at an acceptable level. She was on four different pressure medications, and all of them were being given at the maximum amount allowed.

If the pressors didn't work and Maria couldn't maintain her blood pressure, there was nothing more they could do.

Maria's mother and sister, Sandy and Michelle arrived. They couldn't see Maria right away until the doctor spoke with them. He wanted to make sure they understood the situation and were prepared for what to expect.

The only thing any of us heard was he'd never seen anyone so sick in his years at Brigham. Surviving would be a miracle.

When Michelle was able to see her, she walked straight into the room and spoke to her. "Maria, don't worry. Dad said you're going to be fine."

We don't know if she heard or not, but, Michelle believed he was there for her.

Their father passed away several years ago. When Maria ended up in the hospital, Michelle used to tell her sister she knew their father was watching and would talk about what he was saying.

She never doubted her father was watching Maria.

I know we were all thinking the same thing, even if we hadn't spoken the words.

"I need to wake up from this nightmare. This couldn't be happening. I can't lose her."

Later in the day, Sandy went to our house to be with Carson and Emma. We all knew it wouldn't be easy on them, but they were troopers.

Sandy hoped staying and helping at the house would bring them some normalcy to their days.

We knew this was going to last a while. We didn't know how long. Every day was a gift. We learned to take nothing for granted.

Within the next couple of days, the rest of the family and friends arrived. They helped as much as they could. Michelle offered to take the kids to stay with her in New Jersey. But I didn't want them leaving. I wanted them home when Maria was well enough to be released. She understood and left the invitation open-ended in case I changed my mind.

The children were frightened, and in my opinion, certainly not in an emotional state where they'd be comfortable leaving their mother. I wasn't sure it was in their best interest. I didn't want to make any decisions that would possibly cause problems later.

They were extremely disappointed when they couldn't go to the hospital to see her.

It was heartbreaking.

There were times when the only thing I did was walk around in the daze. Thank God for friends and family. They took up where it was most needed.

We were inundated with offers of help. Our friends checked in daily, asking how Maria was doing, and if we needed them to do anything and offered their assistance.

They were all enormously supportive and kind.

Maria was bloated, pale, and looking extremely frail. The exact opposite of her normal healthy appearance and vivacity. She was unrecognizable. She was hooked up to multiple machines and infusions.

I spoke with Nancee when she came to visit. I could see she was struggling to get her head wrapped around the whole ordeal.

I was on autopilot. There was a glaring helplessness tapping at my conscious, but knew I had to be strong. It was taxing, trying to take it all in, holding it together, and attempting to understand what was going on around me.

Nancee understood the medical jargon and knew the battle Maria was up against. Her body was under attack and the medicines they were pumping into her were to save her life.

They were honest with us; all the lifesaving medication could also cause damage.

I didn't want to believe how critically ill she was. We were all pacing or fidgeting, keyed up and on edge.

Maria's close friend Dianne flew in after I called her. I met her in the hall. I wanted to give her an update and brief warning. I didn't want her walking in and seeing Maria without knowing what to expect.

While she was there, the nurses were monitoring the machines and documenting the results. There wasn't a lot of room. I stayed near the bottom of the bed while Dianne had her moment with Maria.

She asked about the notes taped to the curtain. I explained how it was a list of goals for Maria to reach.

The antibiotics kicked in, and her blood pressure improved. They started removing fluid and cut back on the pressor.

They gave her Amiodarone. Her heart rate and blood pressure stabilized.

Within the first ten days, we were making progress. The next goal was to get her off the pressor, and the fluid removed. It was a slow process.

They were having a hard time keeping the infection under control.

We refused to give in to our fears. We were determined to stay positive. All of us banded together, family and friends. We knew in situations like this it was a necessity to stay positive, grasp onto hope, and continue to support each other.

We'd have our moments to crumble, and then stand back up again and fight. Maria was in an all-out brawl for her life, and we needed to give her all the help she could get.

We rubbed her feet, legs, and arms to help with circulation. Her feet and hands turned purple from lack of blood flow. Eventually, the tips of her toes turned black.

We understood there was a good chance she'd lose her toes, possibly fingers, and maybe her feet. As awful as this sounds, I was grateful. It was a small price to pay…compared to the alternative.

The acid level in her blood decreased. Her PH balance returned to normal. The leaking subsided, and her veins and arteries had gotten stronger.

The doctors took her off the pressor, and Maria continued to maintain her blood pressure.

The next step was getting rid of the fluid buildup. Hooked up to a dialysis machine, they began removing one hundred CCs of fluid per hour. Over the next few days, they increased the removal rate to two hundred CCs per hour.

While in the ICU, they drilled a hole into her right leg. It would be used to put the necessary medications directly into her bone marrow.

Over the weekend, they did a CAT scan. Her throat had an abscess. Her lungs weren't in good shape, her abdominal area was okay, and her brain looked good.

The next several days weren't promising.

Her kidneys were not functioning.

The liver enzymes were elevated and rising.

Her white blood cell count rose.

Maria's lungs were filled with fluid and unable to oxygenate her blood. ECMO put her at the risk because of the use of blood thinners.

She had lactate in her blood.

Her feet and toes were at risk for amputation.

She had sludge in her gallbladder.

They still needed to remove thirteen liters of fluid.

Her digestive system wasn't functioning.

She was on a feeding tube.

She was unconscious and in a medically induced coma.

When she started to become conscious, she became agitated. They had to put something in her mouth to prevent her from biting it.

We couldn't give up. No matter how bad the situation was presented to us, we refused to allow it to take our hope away from us.

We *would* get through this.

Two weeks later:
My social media post

Just talked to my wife!! She is one strong lady. Today is a good day!!

My sister helped keep our friends and family up-to-date. She posted on her social media account Maria's blood pressure was responding to the medications. She let them know she was still on life support for her kidneys and lungs.

"Maria is stable and making steady improvement. She had a CAT scan which did not show any blood flow concerns for her brain. We are happy with her progress and today was another step in the right direction.

"We would like to thank everyone for the overwhelming outpouring of support. We have had a rough few days and have many challenges and a long road ahead, but we feel better today than yesterday and are encouraged by the progress Maria has made thus far. Thanks so much to all the friends and families who have reached out via messages, calls, and texts. Please keep us in your prayers. Thank you Myatt, Maria, Carson, and Emma."

It was awe-inspiring to know there were so many people who prayed for us, who'd helped us, and who wished us well.

July 2014,

Myatt's social media post:

"I have seen so many amazing things. I have met so many amazing people, and learned truly amazing things over the past three weeks. I appreciate all the thoughts and prayers and well wishes everyone has sent over the past few weeks. We are fortunate that, through the grace of God, my wife Maria has shown steady improvement, and we pray for continued progress. Many of our friends and family have asked what they can do for us. We are truly humbled by the support we have already received, and would ask two things of everyone who reads this.

1. Please keep Maria in your prayers as she continues to recover.
2. Please pray for our new friends, Leslie and Lia, and their family. Maria's hospital roommate, Lia, is facing a challenge that thankfully Maria is not right now and Leslie's support for Maria and me over the past week, despite his own situation, is something I could never repay."

Chapter Three

The first week of July, 2014

I barely recall much of what happened in those previous weeks. I was in and out of consciousness. The pain was intense, and when I was awake, I couldn't talk.

Myatt kept vigil, and updated the family on how I was doing and what the doctors were saying.

He sent them videos and pictures of my progress. Maria moving her hand, moving her foot…it was a silly thing, but they were elated and excited about my progress.

He gave as much as information as he could, but even then, it was hard to concentrate.

I wasn't surprised in the least when I learned my lifelong friend, Joanna, was at my side since I was admitted.

It was extremely coincidental she was nearby when all of this happened. She lived in North Carolina and was in the area for a concert.

While in ICU, in one of those not-so-lucid moments, she asked if I remembered her.

How could I *not* remember her?

Another stand-out friend who visited me was Mikki. We had our ups and downs over the years, as many close friends do, but we've always been there for each other.

Once she heard the news of my hospital stay and brush with death, she was at my side. How odd it was to have another coincidence where a friend who was living in Statesboro, Georgia was in Massachusetts. She was traveling to Vermont for her niece's birthday when she heard the news.

Her sister drove her to Boston so she could see me.

One of my closest friends, Dianne, flew in when she received the call from Myatt. She made multiple trips to see me, even though at the time, I didn't know she was there.

After I awoke from the coma, she continued to visit. When I was in rehab, she was a comforting pillar of support. With her there, I felt loved and safe. She was understanding and patient. If I didn't want to talk, she was fine with it, and we sat together in silence.

Many times, she rubbed my feet with gels and creams to help with circulation. It couldn't have been easy considering how black they were and how bad they looked.

The staff who worked with me adored Dianne. At times, they would come in and ask where she was or when she'd be back. She held southern charm in a high stature and kept it there.

Being on as much medication as I was, there were times when my mind was playing tricks on me. I remember insisting that she Google my name and find the picture of me with the University of Georgia mascot.

It didn't faze her. She did it in a way where I didn't suspect I was losing it.

Myatt was there every day and night. He was a rock. He also pushed me so much about my goals and how much there was to do. It was adding stress. I needed a break.

One time, when Dianne was visiting I asked her to tell him not to come. By the strained frustration coming from her eyes, it was obvious she wasn't pleased about the request. She said something to him anyway. I'm sure she managed to say it in a diplomatic way without hurting him.

I must admit. When I get homesick for Georgia, she's front and center.

It couldn't have been easy for her or any of my family and friends.

Mikki sent a card. It was a precious memory from our wedding. The front picture was a black and white photo of me, Myatt, and her. The back had one of the two of us sitting in a big red chair at the Braves Stadium.

It was a daily ritual to look at the photograph. It was a reminder of who I was and what I used to look like.

There were times when it was hard to see the real me. I would look in the mirror and see a stranger. A frail, balding woman with a sunken face and tubes everywhere.

The card helped me stay positive to get back to me.

It was also a great conversation piece. When the nurses and doctors came into the room, they asked about the pictures.

It would break the depressing medical talk and add a bit of cheer to the gloomy room. Unfortunately, reality would creep its way into the corners and crevices of the room whether we liked it or not.

My kidneys weren't functioning. The doctor was positive and confident my kidney functions would return, even though he said nothing was guaranteed.

My liver enzymes were still elevated but were heading in the right direction. I improved enough, and they were able to give me Tylenol to help with the fever.

My white blood cell count was still high, although it wasn't as bad as it was.

My lungs were filled with fluid, and I wasn't able to oxygenate my blood. The lactate in my blood was still present but was starting to be resolved. My feet and toes were still at risk for amputation, although they were slightly improved.

I was taken off the ventilator.

I made up for the lack of communication and talked up a storm with Myatt.

They inserted a drain in my gallbladder to remove the sludge. It was in for about six weeks.

We learned gallbladder sludge was a build-up of crystals, salt, and mucus. It can cause bile to become trapped, which in turn, would cause more complications. It can cause cholecystitis.

The fluid buildup was still an issue.

I was able to have some ginger ale swabs when they took me off the ventilator. It wasn't the frappe I was asking for, but I figured it was better than nothing.

Myatt told me about the odd things I said while I was out of it. For some unknown reason, I was mad at my friend because she made fun of pregnant women and bad-mouthed FedEx.

He said I was furious at Allie and never wanted to talk to her again. Who knows why? I'm not sure what was going through my head while I was in a coma. We were all baffled about that one.

I was upset with Myatt because he was using Apple TV to project an image of his face on the wall.

I wanted to go bra shopping.

I was completely convinced I had pictures of a news reporter with bulldogs, and I wanted him to find the pictures.

The best request…I asked him to get in bed and snuggle, and said maybe we could do some *shenanigans*.

Interesting what meds can do.

They put tunnel lines to assist my kidneys.

My liver enzymes were still elevated but they were heading in the right direction. We were told my liver improved 70% from where it was.

They x-rayed my lungs. Unsatisfied with what they found, I was put back on the ventilator. They wanted to put in a trach because I was intubated so long.

I was hoping to avoid it and the extra hole in my body. We were really excited I was taken off the ventilator and told several people. Being put on the trach was discouraging.

I was going to survive. Nothing else mattered.

On a more positive note, they put a tube in my nose, and I was able to eat and drink with the trach. For a while, I was on a tube feed.

The lactate in my blood was resolving.

After they put the tunnel line in, there was an issue with the trach. I had some bleeding in my lungs. They removed it. I was back to being intubated with sedation and without the trach.

It was a setback.

The doctor didn't know what caused the bleeding. They scheduled a procedure to go down into my lungs with a scope to look around and suction up any blood.

A few days later, the tracheostomy was done. All went well, and I was moved back to my room. I learned how to use a speaking valve. It was frustrating and difficult. My voice was raspy due to the trach.

Swallowing is an instinct. We do it without thinking, until something happens, making you conscious of an issue. My natural reflex was no longer available to me. It wasn't working the way it was supposed to and anxiety reared its tendons.

I squashed the panic from the sensation of choking. It was a battle to keep myself calm and forcibly slow my heart beat and labored breathing.

Because of the trouble I had swallowing, solid foods weren't allowed until I could strengthen my muscles. Due to the length of time I was intubated, I lost muscle strength in my throat. I needed to exercise my throat muscles.

All of my muscles were weak. I couldn't hold my cell phone. It felt like a heavy brick slab. It made it difficult to communicate through text.

Myatt brought a dry erase board for me to use for communicating with him and the staff. I had a hard time using it. I was writing my letters on top of each other. He wrote out the alphabet and I pointed so he knew what I needed.

In mid-July, on the same day I was moved to Spaulding Rehab Hospital, I finally got to see the children. I was worried about how they'd react, but they were troopers.

It was a much needed ray of gladness that settled in my heart. It gave me the incentive and courage to move forward. I knew it was going to be a long road ahead.

The next goal was to wean me off the vent, pass the swallow test, and do physical and occupational therapy so I could go home.

Who thinks about all these things? I didn't until I had to use them and the ability wasn't there.

After the first swallow test, thick liquids were my choices for breakfast, lunch and dinner menu. I relearned how to eat. I had to tuck my chin to avoid choking, and getting fluids in my lungs. I couldn't have anything too watery, or I coughed and choked. The liquid would also get into my lungs, which in turn, would cause more problems.

Eating was a chore as well as talking. Yes, talking became something to practice. I never realized how many throat muscles we use to speak!

Physical and occupational therapy became a part of my life.

I was determined to regain my strength, get off dialysis, and defeat the bladder and urinary infection, which refused to behave itself.

I was tired, grumpy, and extremely hard-headed. I snapped at a few of the nurses.

For goodness sake, I was sleeping! Did they *really* need to wake me to check my vitals?

I used to think, *wake up, I need to give you your sleeping pill* was a joke. Nope, not a joke.

And a shower would've been lovely!

When my mother would visit, she washed my face, and used a washcloth on my hair. She sat in the bed, and we snuggled. I could rest secure in her arms.

She was the comfort I needed.

Myatt was the head coach for our son Carson's baseball team. The team and their families' love, kindness, and prayers were highly appreciated. We are fortunate to be a part of such a great group of people.

The boys posted a picture with a sign. *We miss you, Maria.*

Sitting in the hospital, I had plenty of time for serious thinking.

The days were rough. The PT and OT were exhausting, add the dialysis to it, and I was ripe for an argument.

It was one of those, *go ahead, piss me off…I dare you*, moods. Unfortunately, it lasted longer than a day.

I can't imagine how many people swallowed back angry retorts. They should be awarded angel's wings for their kindness and patience.

I was reaching the point where I only needed the ventilator for a few hours at night. I'd come a long way.

I hated rehab. There wasn't anything wrong with the people who worked there. I loathed everything about it. It was a horrible reminder of my demise and lack of independence.

Battling depression and constantly upset, my drive to stay positive was an incessant test of faith.

I was visiting with Myatt and the children, and we were talking and chatting about everyday family things. My head was itchy and I found a scab on the back of my head. I pulled on it and a clump of hair dangled from my fingers.

I was mortified. I was lying in bed for so long I got sores and scabs on my scalp. On top of my body going through all the trauma, it was effecting my skin and scalp.

Who would've imagined I would start losing my hair, too?

All I wanted was to eat and go home.

There were times when I refused to do the physical and occupational therapy, which only made things worse and took longer to get better.

On the upside, I was allowed to go outside. I loved being outside.

While I was fighting the depression, and forcing myself to take therapy, the group we hung out with on Friday nights came to see me.

I remember this day like it was yesterday. They arrived with positive attitudes and genuine smiles. I was given a few pairs of new jammies. It's one of my favorite gifts to get and one of my favorite things to buy.

I had a great visit with them and felt so optimistic about things until we went back up to my floor. The doctor sat me down and said he wasn't satisfied with my white blood cell count.

The invisible Acme anvil fell on my joyous moment. I could hear the crash reverberating in my brain. It was cruel, ruthless joke.

I was sent back to the hospital.

When I was admitted to the ER, they thought my white blood count spiked because of my toes. They believed the toes were causing the issues and needed to be amputated immediately.

It felt like a million doctors came in and out of the room. With it being a teaching hospital, multiple groups came in and asked the same types of questions.

I was being difficult. They wouldn't let me eat, and I was famished.

The vascular doctor came and spoke with us. My uncle, who's an orthopedic surgeon, was there as well. He helped us understand what we were being told.

It was the first time I saw Myatt break down. He kept apologizing to me. He believed it was his fault I'd be losing my toes.

I remember reassuring him, saying it was just a few toes.

Once I was admitted, they ran a bunch of tests, and I also had dialysis.

I was looking forward to the swallow test, and anticipating having my trach downsized.

Everyone irritated me. As far as I was concerned, people couldn't breathe right. The world around me was one humongous tornado, and it wouldn't stop storming.

I became more despondent and angry. I was extremely unreasonable.

I hadn't had water or anything to drink since being admitted. I was in rehab and was told a therapist was working with me on practicing swallowing. They would determine if I was ready to do a swallow test.

I snapped at the nurses and therapists. I didn't recall practicing swallowing. I ended up back in the hospital and they moved my dialysis appointment to the afternoon. I would definitely be getting my swallow test done in the morning.

They came for dialysis, and I pitched a fit. I was furious. They said they'd do the swallow test. The schedule for the test was canceled because I had to have dialysis. I was told they only schedule a limited amount, and I'd be up for the next scheduling session.

I wasn't happy, and I made sure they knew it. I was so frustrated I couldn't sleep.

One thing I learned while I was staying at the hospital, I needed to speak up. Persistence is a necessity. Especially with my fluctuating moods, there were times when I made sure there was no doubt, whatsoever, about what I wanted. They heard me.

The doctors did a comprehensive search for an infection. They were thinking the white blood cell count was elevated because I was confined for so long. It was most likely caused by the swelling and decomposing toes on my feet.

While I was there, I ended up getting diarrhea. The abnormal intestinal issues, fluid stools, and gas pains were caused by dehydration.

None of this improved my disposition.

They did an MRI and the swallow test on the same day.

I prayed I'd pass. If I passed the swallow test, I'd be close to the end of this long disastrous tunnel.

I didn't pass the swallow test...sort of. I was allowed nectar thick liquids. I drank through a straw with my chin tucked down to avoid aspirating.

Thickened liquids have no taste. Wait, let me rephrase with blatant honesty. They taste horrible.

After practicing drinking thickened liquids through a straw, one of the physician assistant's went to the rehab and asked them to thin out my drinks. So refreshing!

It was a step forward.

While I was in the hospital, I started walking more with my walker. I was regaining a spot of independence. It was a positive progression to be able to take care of myself after using the restroom.

One of the therapists who came to work with me at the rehab center had me practicing sipping water from a Dixie cup. I hadn't had a drink in almost seven weeks.

I cried when she said I could have the water. I was in disbelief. It was embarrassing. I was a 40-year-old woman crying because I got to drink a cup of water.

She explained I needed to drink slowly.

But that wasn't happening. Nope, not at all.

This may sound silly, but I let spit build up in my mouth, tuck my chin and swallow. I figured muscle repetition. The more I pictured myself and my muscles swallowing, the better off I would be. As I continued practicing and drinking with the Dixie cup, she put me on a schedule for the swallow test.

I was ready.

I was excited and nervous because if I failed, there was a waiting period before I could try again.

The doctor and his assistant were so nice to me. I was emotional and anxious while I was taking the test.

I kept asking, "Did I pass? Did it look good?"

I passed!

I couldn't wait to drink water and eat food, real honest to goodness delicious food.

The water was *so* good. It was refreshing, and hit the spot. I was craving foods, but regardless of what I was eating, none of it was enjoyable or satisfied me.

Myatt brought a ton of food. He ordered all of my favorites from any restaurant I wanted. The goody bag from home was filled with foods he was sure I enjoyed: Cereal bars, grits, oatmeal, and snacks.

I didn't want any of it. I started drinking Ensure to meet my calorie count. If I consumed the required daily calories, and eat solid foods, they'd take my tube out. I ate a lot of baked potatoes and green beans.

My next goal was to get the feeding tube out.

I hated that thing!

I struggled to eat anything other than pudding, blueberries, mashed potatoes and green beans.

The dialysis and fluid removal hadn't cleaned my blood. Nevertheless, my lab tests showed improvement. After several weeks of dialysis, my kidneys began to slowly function again. I had to wait for them to work properly, and only then, could I get the dialysis line out.

Around the beginning of August, they took out the gallbladder drain.

At this point, the *worry list* dwindled.

It was time to take the tube feed out of my nose. Another crossroad passed.

On the day the tube was coming out, I asked the doctor if it would hurt. She said no. She removed tubes on a regular basis, and never had trouble.

She was wrong!

Because I had previously pulled mine out, they put an anchor on mine so it wouldn't happen again.

My aunt held my hand as the doctor pulled it out. There was blood everywhere.

The curdling scream was ear-piercing. I swear they heard me three miles away.

I hadn't called my husband right away. I wanted it to be a surprise when he came in to see me.

I didn't know he was able to see my progress online. I was disappointed. My eyes watered, and my chest constricted. Someone popped all of my *I did it* balloons.

I wanted to be the one who told him I wasn't going to be on dialysis anymore.

Once the dialysis line was out, I could go home.

Next on the agenda: How to care for my feet.

Chapter Four

Emma's seventh birthday arrived and I was despondent. I was going to miss her party. First thing in the morning, Myatt brought her to the rehab hospital to see me.

It was important for us, and myself, to give her the special gift together.

She wanted a computer like her brother's, and we decided to let her have one.

Myatt had a fantastic party for her. It was probably one of the best she's ever had. He gave our friend, Millie, his credit card and let her plan the celebration.

The thing to do back then was to make bath salts and lotions. Emma was thrilled. Millie arranged to have the party at Bath Junkie, and the kids made their own bath crafts.

My little precious princess wore a brand new dress and tiara. Everyone tried to make it an extraordinary and memorable day for her. They wanted to keep her occupied and cheerful.

I expected and encouraged my brother, Johnny, to go to Emma's party, but he wanted to spend the day with me.

I love my brother dearly, but I was concerned about how I would entertain him. It's not like I could get up and do anything.

When we were younger, he and my sister were close. She was the tomboy, and I was the odd-man-out.

I worried he'd be bored to tears and couldn't get out of there fast enough.

Boy, was I wrong!

Johnny took me outside, out of my claustrophobic room, and away from the constant noise of rehab. I hadn't realized how much I needed it.

I never knew how much my brother loved me until that day.

It was an eye-opener. He said we could do whatever I wanted. He brought his iPad, which for him was a big deal. He's dreadfully particular about his things. No one touches his stuff, including me.

He rubbed my back when I was getting anxious. We watched television together.

We went for walks.

One outdoor expedition took us to a bit of a rough moment. I was hooked to my tube feed and we were outside. I had to get back to the room…fast. As we rushed back to my room, I squeezed the hole holding my feed tube between my legs.

I have to admit this is a bit embarrassing. I mulled back and forth, on whether I should add this explanation. However, I gave in, knowing I wanted to be as honest as possible.

I recently started being able to use the bathroom facilities on my own. I wore depends and was tired of having accidents.

The tube feed, at times, made me feel nauseous, my stomach would churn, and physical discomfort would set in. Whenever I felt the urge to relieve myself, I hurried to the bathroom to avoid any mishaps.

I understand it's a bodily function, but I didn't want it to happen anywhere but my room. I preferred to avoid any issues and embarrassment.

All in all, it was one of the best days I've spent with Johnny. I never again doubted how much my brother loved me.

I was going home.

There was such a relief when I said those words. A ton of weight lifted off my shoulders.

I triumphed and beaten the river of death, but the struggles were merely beginning.

The first instruction for my home care:
Walking as tolerated.

I used to run. I was in great shape…and now it was, walking as tolerated. Every time I saw those words, I wanted to bust out in wailing, wallowing tears.

I needed help with all normal activities. They were taken for granted. I'm not exaggerating.

I had all I needed to keep mobile: a walker, my husband, and my family…

I wouldn't have been able to do any of it without them. They were there to assist me from morning ablutions, to getting dressed, and eating, to name a few.

I was a person who was physically fit. It was difficult to deal with needing assistance to stand and stay balanced on my feet.

It was an inner battle against being viciously angry or bitter. I looked in the mirror and saw a different person. The mirror spoke volumes. I had reminders, and still do, of every battle I have fought to be where I am now.

I knew I should be grateful to be alive. Nevertheless, I was stubborn and didn't want to see or talk to anyone.

Considering no one really understood what I went through or what I was going through, I certainly didn't want to listen to anyone's advice. They didn't get it, and they needed to leave me alone.

I, of course being who I am, had to get the most dangerous and deadly kind. Why would I do anything half way?

Sepsis isn't talked about and when it is, it's often referred to incorrectly as blood poisoning. We hear of people dying of infections, but often it's really sepsis.

I had all of the symptoms but didn't know it was sepsis. I didn't even know what it was. The rash on my stomach spread to my extremities. I had strep throat, and was clueless about it leading to anything else, or was possibly a sign of a bigger problem.

Ever since I was pregnant with Emma, I had a hard time drinking water. The dark urine, which I assumed was merely dehydration, was a sign of my kidneys starting to shut down.

How did I miss that?

My enemy, the sepsis, the streptococcal toxic shock, the heart attack, the renal failure, and the amputations of five toes on one foot and four on the other, had all scored one for my foe. My feet were one big web…with no defined toes.

I fought through the clammy hands, racing heart, terror sweats and the wobbly legs. It didn't matter how much I cried, how much pain I was in, or how angry I was, I wasn't giving up.

The beast wasn't going to beat me.

I refused to just exist. I needed to live.

We only get one chance in life.

I transformed into a different person. Out of the ashes, a new and improved Maria emerged. Along with all other clichés I can come up with, it's the best one.

Honestly, I'm surprised the ant song wasn't in my head more often.

High hopes…she's got high hopes. She's got hot apple pie in the sky hope.

There were other songs that mulled around in my head. I used them to keep fighting, and to prevent myself from being a royal B. I preferred my husband, my kids, and my family not hate me because I morphed into an absolutely unreasonable shrew.

The problem with always being angry? I couldn't see truth and reality. I became blinded. I didn't want to be a bitter, choleric person.

I wanted to be positive and free of this burden.

Although, I bow my head and freely admit, I did lose it sometimes. They'll all attest to my confessions of arbitrary behavior, but they'll also say they understood.

I would win this battle and be happy again.

Who would've thought a strep infection would lead to a gangrenous foot? Or cholecystitis and needing a cholecystectomy tube for my gall bladder?

At home and at PT and OT (physical and occupational therapy), I worked on my mobility, endurance, and work toward functional independence. I learned, faster than anyone could imagine, how much I needed toes to walk and balance.

We also needed to learn how to properly clean and dress the wounds. Bathing and avoiding moisture or wetness was a challenge. Regardless of how well we protected my feet, I was terrified of getting them wet.

Panic and anxiety slipped in more often than I like to admit.

As the weeks moved forward, my therapy sessions continued. I got stronger. I was able to move around without a chair, walk up a flight of stairs, and stand longer.

Considering we had a two-story house, walking up a flight of stairs was an event to celebrate.

Who would've believed a major accomplishment would be scheduling an appointment for shoes to help walk, support and increase my mobility and help with foot drop.

The *doom doctors* told me I'd never run again. It was hard enough dealing with the amputations. The emotional struggles were unnerving. I had to deal with the loss of my toes, and knew I'd be disabled for the rest of my life.

I was my own adversary, and I wasn't going to allow that part of me to hold myself down. Fine, I would be disabled and may have a gait.

It didn't stop me from believing I could run again.

There must've been something confrontational in my brain. I refused to accept their negative pronouncements.

They said I couldn't.

I set out to prove them wrong.

No matter how many times the *doom doctors*, the naysayers, and all the specialists warned I'd never run again, it made me that much more determined. I would keep seeing more doctors until I found one who said I could run again.

I didn't care if I needed more surgery. I didn't care if I needed more physical and occupational therapy.

I refused to give up hope.

There were many times when things started getting better and agony reared its ugly head. My feet and ankles would have sharp stinging pains, and I would have to go back and start again.

Those setbacks brought me to the people who believed I could get better and possibly run again. I was taken to the doctors, nurses, and therapists who would eventually help me through this ordeal. They were as determined and stubborn as I was.

I fought for my goals, even when all the medical experts said it'd be hopeless.

I refused to consider submitting to defeat. This would not be my downfall.

Chapter Five

On August 8, 2014, I watched a video of my son, Carson, accepting the ALS ice bucket challenge…

And I went home.

I was told I was being released from the rehab hospital!
If I could've danced, I would've been doing it up and down the hallways.
Myatt and I wanted to surprise the children and called my aunt to let her know and have the kids stay up past their bedtime. We swore her to secrecy. I love my uncle dearly, but he's horrible at keeping secrets, especially good news. He gets excited about having news he tends to blurt out information and spread the word as quickly as possible.

Myatt's social media post:
"7 weeks, 2 days, 9 hours… Tonight officially ends the longest Dr. visit of our lives. Welcome home, Maria Papalia-Meier."

Leaving the rehab facility wasn't easy. They tried to take my dialysis line out, and it didn't work. The sheer trauma was enough to blindside anyone. The attendant was having a hard time…
I wouldn't have been released if it wasn't for my nurse, Kelly. She was absolutely awesome and was the one who'd been a positive, driving force for my ultimate liberation.

I am a Runner

After the issues were resolved, we headed toward the elevator. Kelly came out of another patient's room and asked for a goodbye hug. She was surprised I wasn't happier.

I explained what happened when they removed the line. I was drained from the procedure, irritated, and had a pounding headache.

Nevertheless, I was overjoyed. I was leaving.

I never saw Kelly again. Like we did with the ICU nurses, I wanted to return and thank her for all she did.

I waited until I could walk in and look normal. She wasn't there. It was disappointing. I didn't want to miss anyone.

The first night home, I posted on Myatt's social media page. It was quiet at home, and it was disconcerting. It wasn't noisy at the facilities, but there were always sounds: Machines, hushed, muted voices, a television, and someone over the speaker calling a doctor or nurse.

All I wanted to do was go to my room and lay down. I was too exhausted. I was choked up with relief and was having several moments filled with mixed emotions. There was a wrenching dread something would go wrong, and I'd end up back in the hospital.

I had a rush of elation because I was home. I was sad and confused. My eyes filled with tears from fear and happiness. I was an emotional mess.

Obviously, I was delighted to be home and see the kids.

It was nice and a little scary. The lack of beeps and buzzing meant no machines, and no one checking my vitals. I was watched, babied, and coddled. After having constant supervision for over seven weeks, I was on my own.

The TV in our room looked huge in comparison to the small set in my hospital room. It was all familiar and unfamiliar at the same time.

I was home.

I was adamant about leaving all signs of my stay behind me. I didn't want anything reminding me I wasn't healed yet.

There was talk of a hospital bed downstairs, which I immediately squashed. The shower chair was a definite *no*.

During one of my surgeries, they drilled into my leg. It hit a nerve and possibly damaged a muscle. It caused drop foot. I was unable to flex my foot up and down. We worked on strengthening the area at the rehab facility, and PT.

I agreed to the walker.

It was a concession and a necessity. I'd be able to walk without tripping over my own feet. If I fell in the middle of the night, it would've been terrifying.

I didn't want to end up reversing my progress. I certainly didn't want to return to the hospital because of something so silly, nor over anything which could've been avoided.

Chapter Six

The gauntlet was thrown. The challenged accepted, and conquered.

The Goal? September 1st. Myatt and the children wanted me home for his birthday. I made it.

I was wearing huge surgical shoes and a bandaged leg, but we did it.

Myatt and I went out for dinner, and a marvelous time. It was the first time we went out alone together since I was home.

I rocked it in my long and baggy pants.

The first week of September, I had an appointment with the vascular doctor. We received practical and positive feedback.

My feet were healing the way they needed to be. We asked for a second opinion for my toes, and she put in the request.

Even though my feet hurt and had a burning sensation, it was all good news. We stayed optimistic about the outcome.

I kept hopeful eyes looking up-ward. It's the little things I accomplished. Most people would consider it silly, but I figured out how to wash my hair by myself!

The end of September we celebrated our thirteenth wedding anniversary. 2014 was a rough one. It was also the year we proved to ourselves how much we really loved and needed each other.

We are blessed.

It was important to learn and accept my life, and improve the way I was looking at it. I didn't want to die. I wanted to live a long, healthy life.

It wasn't merely wanting to live. It was adding precious and wonderful memories to the years I'd be living. I wanted to be optimistic and upbeat, and I wanted my years ahead to be happy and promising.

I looked forward to spending my elder years with Myatt. Not necessarily sharing each other's dentures in a soaking tray but close.

I was seeing a vascular surgeon who was with Brigham and excelled at what he did. He had absolutely no bedside manner.

We were in his office when he informed us he didn't think my feet were going to get any better. It was time to schedule surgery.

He wanted to perform a metatarsal amputation on my feet. If we accepted his advice, I would've been left with less than what I have now.

Myatt and I requested a second opinion. We were referred to an orthopedic doctor who specialized in feet and ankles.

We made an appointment. After examining my feet, the orthopedic physician de-bred them. De-breeding is the removal of dead tissue. He used scissors and cut at the black on my feet.

I acted like it seriously hurt. Honestly, it was unsettling. He reprimanded me with pretty strong words. I won't forget. It was a stony and cruel much needed metaphorical slap.

With a stern look, he said. "Don't say it hurts if it doesn't. Sometimes, doctors can only guess how much pain you're in by your reactions. If you exaggerate, you could lose more of your foot than necessary. No one will want to touch you."

I was stunned, but he wasn't finished.

"You need to find a way to make it through the appointments for de-breeding your toes. Either take medication, or go see someone who'll help you with the anxiety."

If I wanted to hold onto the hope of keeping my toes, I couldn't over-exaggerate the pain and discomfort.

I had to be honest, and keep my apprehension at bay.

I was crying and upset. He didn't care. While he was cutting, he did admit he didn't know how it felt to go through what I did.

It was jarring to hear his harsh words. He was a callous, insensitive jerk. My bruised emotions and feelings were as wounded as my feet.

He was right. I may not have wanted to hear those words, but it obviously needed to be said. In his cold, hard-love way, he did me a lot of good. It was a crucial push toward my recovery and healing.

I called my regular physician and requested a prescription for anxiety medication.

Myatt and I traveled every week to the wound center in Boston to have my feet and leg worked on. Our neighbor, Leigh Ann, took the kids at six in the morning, so we could travel to Boston for my appointments.

It became a weekly routine the children began to enjoy. She was there for my family when we needed her the most. We'll never be able to repay her for all she did.

It was interesting how coincidental it was considering my neighbor's name in Atlanta was Leigh Ann, and then of course, this Leigh Ann. Both of them were a godsend.

Leigh Ann, in Atlanta, was also a superb friend. I couldn't have made it without her steadfast help with the children. She helped take care of them when I traveled for work. She picked them up, took them to daycare, and at times, her stepdaughter watched them if I had an overnight job.

Struggling to keep a positive attitude was, at times, easy or, at a flip of the coin, daunting. I had so much positive reinforcement coming at me, yet, there were moments that kept slapping me in the face.

I was disheartened because I was supposed to run in the half-marathon with Leigh Ann. It was an emotional time. I was angry, jealous, left out, and downright appalled at my resentment. I know she was disappointed, and I wanted her to run.

Why should she lose out because I couldn't run?

I needed to support and encourage her, certainly not whine and bemoan my fate.

I remember joking around when I came home. I was walking around in my big orthotic shoes and announced. "I can run."

Since I couldn't run, there was a spot in the race. I asked Dawn to run in my place.

While I was in the ICU, they drilled into my right leg, which allowed the medicines to enter directly into my bone marrow. It left a blood blister below my leg. It eventually surfaced and became a large scab. We were told to leave it alone. It was the body's way of creating a natural bandage.

The physician at the wound clinic didn't agree. The scab was removed on the first visit. He put numbing medication around the wound, took the scissors, and cut it off. When he was done, the hole was so deep I could see my bone.

They packed it with gauze soaked in saline. Then, they started working on my toes. Cutting the black off and looking for new tissue growth.

I took my anxiety and pain medication in the car when we got close to Brigham. I found a way of coping, not necessarily, what the doctor recommended, but it worked for me.

I squirmed and wanted to rebel. I hid my head, covered my eyes, or wore sunglasses so I couldn't see what they were doing. A few times, I listened to music so I couldn't hear what was said.

I was petrified. My pinky toes were dead. There wasn't any hope left to save them. It was obvious they weren't coming back.

When the nurse came to the house to change my bandages, I covered my face. I didn't want to see them.

At the wound center, they took my bandages off for examination. I held my breath and prayed my poor toes wouldn't fall off into their hands.

The whole process sucked. Yes, I said it. It sucked. I could add a few more colorful metaphors, but I'm sure everyone knows what I mean.

I was squeamish and cowardly. The courage wasn't there. I didn't want to see and didn't want to know.

As long as I didn't see them, it couldn't happen.

I know it was wrong. I knew it then, and I know it now. But I didn't want to face reality.

Life has its ups and downs. I understand that. I wanted the disastrous nightmare to take a break. I wanted to scream. *Please stop. I can't take anymore. Leave me alone!*

But the fighter hung on.

My feet bled through the bandages causing them to stick to my wounds. Each time, they sprayed my feet with saline. Little by little, inch-by-inch, they carefully and meticulously peeled the bandages away from the wound.

The doctor made a concerted effort not to hurt me. He wasn't as gentle as the nurse, and it increased my anxiety. As gentle as they were, my feet would still be pretty sore.

Maria Papalia-Meier

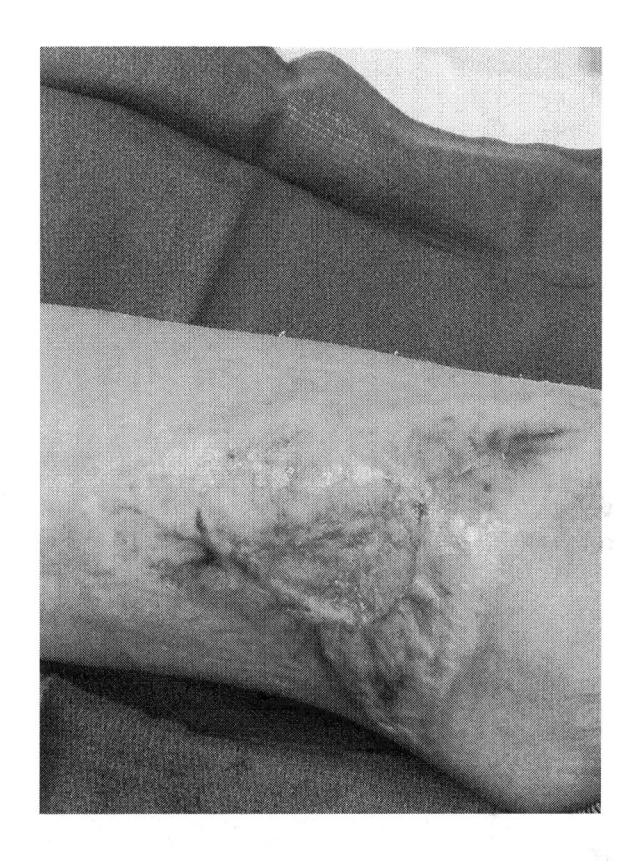

I was lucky. My fingers worked fine and they only had to concentrate on my feet and knee. Who would believe they were once black and were able to recover so well?

The human body is an incredible thing.

We couldn't avoid it any longer. The surgical procedure was scheduled to amputate my toes. A skin graft was set up for my knee in October.

Modern technology is astounding. They've given me so much in return for such a devastating loss.

After the amputation was done, I couldn't look at my toes for a while. One night Myatt was changing my bandages. He was inspecting the stitches and wounds for issues. The doctor and nurse explained what to expect, and any unusual signs to look for.

I held a pillow over my head so I wouldn't see my feet. Carson was standing in the bedroom doorway and said, "Mom, they don't look bad at all. You should look."

I did, and he was right. I looked at my new reality. It wasn't as bad as I thought.

Later in the evening, Myatt said the look on Carson's face was contrary to his encouraging words. My nine year old little man was being strong for me, and wanted to give me the reassurance he obviously realized I needed.

What a wise young man!

It was a well-earned lesson. In the face of adversity, my boy stood tall. His resolve to face it and encourage me was a gift I have kept close to the heart and always cherish.

We were warned it might take up to a year for the swelling and healing to work its magic. I could deal with the situation ahead.

There were a few, not-so-proud moments filled with unnecessary and exaggerated anxiety. Shower time was most enjoyable for anyone who loved listening to a shrieking, shrewish, panicky woman. Just a bit of sarcasm there, in case you missed that…

Taking a shower was a dreadful project. I wasn't supposed to get my feet wet.

Period.

It took Myatt about an hour to prepare me. We put on tall waterproof bags used for covering casts and bandages. I lost so much weight they weren't tight enough on my legs. Myatt wrapped the top of them with waterproof tape.

We took every precaution available to us. It didn't matter. I was still paranoid.

The first time I ended up staying in the shower for about five minutes. I freaked out and was terrified they were getting wet.

I wailed in terror. "I'm going to lose my feet! They can't get wet."

After each shower we had to remove the bags and make sure my feet were 100% dry. They couldn't be rewrapped with bandages if there was any dampness whatsoever.

This process took an exceedingly long time. To say I had high anxiety then was a complete understatement. I couldn't have anything else happen to me.

I couldn't lose my feet, too!

This was hard on Myatt. I saw the strain in his clenched jaw. His patience was perfection. I remember him talking about when he spoke to the doctors about bringing me home. He wanted me there no matter what had to be done. A wheelchair wouldn't be an issue. He meant it.

Did he know how absolutely unreasonable I would be? Probably. I was angry, nauseated with guilt, and felt the fool…

The man deserves the highest award for the most patient husband in the universe. He didn't merely have to deal with my physical needs, but my emotional waves of angry outbursts, and frustrations.

Like my mother when my father was bedridden, Myatt worked all day, took care of the children, and took care of me.

It's a wonder he only got a bit snippy and short-tempered. I'm telling you, my husband rocks!

Chapter Seven

Christmas was always a big deal for our family and me. When I was a kid, Christmas Eve included all of my cousins, aunts, and uncles. We usually had at least thirty-five people who celebrated with us.

Myatt and I traveled between Iowa and New York for the holidays. We alternated years with each family.

There may have only been a couple of times we couldn't travel. When we were living in Atlanta, Carson was due in January. I wasn't allowed to travel far from home.

Our neighbors down the street invited us to spend the holiday with them. It helped, and I didn't feel so forlorn without being with family for the holiday.

We resumed our holiday travels. It wasn't easy, but it was important to be with family at Christmas time. I wanted the kids to experience what I did as a child.

When we went to New York and Iowa, the kids were with family and cousins. Myatt and I have two different family traditions. Depending on whose home we visited for the year, we followed their traditions.

Traveling during the holidays was stressful, but we made it an adventure. We put them in their PJs, and they watched old Christmas movies.

Most of the time coming home from Iowa we spent Christmas night in a hotel and the kids would get a special present from the ladies at the front desk.

It was a lot, but it was fun. We were with family, and it was the only thing that mattered.

When the 2014 Christmas holiday season approached, we knew it was going to be a hard one. It'd be the first time we'd spend the holiday with only the four of us.

There was no way I could travel. It was disheartening. I certainly didn't need anything encouraging despondency.

The holidays were so important. My mother and brother offered to come and spend Christmas with us.

I worried about my mother coming. The weather could be a feisty cantankerous creature. She didn't like driving in the snow. I completely understood. She'd be coming from upstate New York. It was over a five-hour drive with too many opportunities for a dangerous weather change.

I needed to stay positive.

Emma and I were sitting by the fireplace listening to the familiar crackle of the warm logs. She was helping me write Christmas cards.

She exclaimed, "Momma! They're so nice. They gave us envelopes, too."

She addressed the envelopes. I added the little notes, and signed the cards. It was a pleasant moment. She was a huge help. I love hanging out with my little bean.

I was chatting with my friend, Nancee, and told her how upset I was about the holiday. She offered to come over Christmas morning.

I was totally blown away.

With a little inspiration, I sent out an invitation to our old crew. We ended up with a group of about thirty people, including kids.

Everyone brought their favorite Christmas morning food. I was responsible for the coffee, mimosas, and hash browns. No one wanted me to do too much.

It has become our yearly tradition, and we love it. We celebrate Christmas at our house and our families rotate the years and join us for the holidays.

New Year's came along, and we wished and prayed for a happy and healthy new year.

I posted to my friends and family on social media. I wanted to make sure they knew how much I loved and appreciated them.

"I wish all my friends and family a safe and blessed New Year. I am blessed to be here this year, and if I have learned anything from my experience, it is to live life to the fullest, never miss an opportunity to tell someone how much you love them, and take time to spend with your family. Life gets busy, but there is nothing more important than being with the ones you love. Here's to a fabulous 2015!!!!!"

Chapter Eight

It's those thoughtful gifts from loved ones that brighten the day. As a special surprise, Emma made me custom-made flip flops for people with no toes. How awesome is that?

Myatt has a peculiar sense of humor I adore. It has helped with the down moments on more occasions than I can count.

One particular memory was of him getting into my phone and playing around with the auto-correct. Whenever I typed great, it sent Fabu!

We played heads-up, an app from The Ellen Show. We played with different categories. One of us held the iPad above our head while the team players gave clues of the word. My cheeks and belly hurt from laughing so hard. It was such a long time, much of it at my own expense!

It was a blast. I highly recommend the game for a good, hearty laugh with friends and family.

It kept much-needed smiles on their faces, especially because of my restricted activity and mobility.

By mid-January, the doctors and I were pleased with my progress. My feet were healing well. As warned, I developed blisters. An appointment with the podiatrist was scheduled to fit for shoes and insoles.

At the wound center, we met with a podiatrist who was able to prescribe orthotics. It's a special insert made for your shoe, and helped tremendously. It helped my balance, avoid foot-sliding, and kept my foot positioned in the correct location in the shoe.

He also gave recommendations on shoes I can wear. The only negative — I had to wear shoes even around the house. No barefoot walking for a while.

I liked walking around barefoot. It was an adjustment period. I kept reminding myself, it was all temporary.

One of the frustrating morning ablutions was the constant battle with my hair. It started to grow back in again and was no longer falling out. Because of the irregular growth, it was too short and uneven.

My stylist was a miracle worker! She created inventive ways of trimming my hair to experimenting with different colors. For fun, there were a few times when we highlighted my thin locks with pink, blonde, and purples.

Myatt and I discussed buying a wig. My hair had gotten so thin, along with multiple bald spots. I wore thick headbands and bandanas to cover the top of my head.

I was a sexy biker chick with bald spots!

When I was younger, it was very curly. Like most young girls, I hated it. I didn't want all those curls.

It flabbergasted me when I heard about women who paid hundreds of dollars to have curly hair.

I have complete sympathy now for women with balding or bad hair. As I watched the new growth, I was relieved to see it was healthy, undamaged, and with curls.

Once in a while Myatt would comment about not liking women with curly hair. I would eye the shiny skin on top of his head, and respond, "I don't like bald men."

I received my orthopedic sneakers and was thrilled. I couldn't tell you enough how absolutely amazing and comfortable they were. I could've sworn Tinkerbell sprinkled me with pixie dust and a million sparkles of sunshine.

While wearing the shoes, I kept an eye on any chafing against my skin and feet. I practiced using them, and gradually acclimated to the shoes and the prosthetic inlays.

It was a long road, winding, bumpy, and full of potholes. Sheer and utter fortitude kept me moving forward. The love and support from my family and friends was an inspiration.

I never knew how much I missed the daily things, nor how much they would change. I took my cheery, normal days for granted, and then this happened. It was a wake-up call. Not merely for myself, but for everyone around me.

If physical strength was the cat's meow, I was in deep trouble.

I had none.

This monster was huge. Even if his hands were tied behind his back, and I had boxer's gloves on, I couldn't beat him. He'd win, hands down.

I was drained.

I learned it wasn't only physical strength keeping me moving. It was sheer willpower.

I had the hope and motivation to fight back. With all ninety-plus pounds, I was going to pulverize this beast, and beat him back into the corner where he belonged. It didn't matter how drained or vulnerable I was. I wasn't going to surrender.

Then another setback. I assumed the emotional bruising was over. I was faced with another challenge.

Back in the hospital I went.

Surgery was needed because I developed a MRSA infection in the bone of my left foot. I was scheduled for an afternoon appointment, but there was an opening, and they pushed me back to the morning. They removed five more bones from my left foot.

While infirmed, I learned my constant cravings for pizza became my comfort food.

Pizza's good. I like it!

At least I wasn't craving beets...

I was so ready to be back to normal. I began to believe there was no such thing in my future. It was a three steps forward, four steps back scenario. My body was stuck in reverse, and it was calamitous.

Myatt posted to our family and friends on his social media page.

"Surgery went fine, and she's recovering. Love this hospital, but would be glad to not see it again for a very long time."

Yes, me too. It wasn't meant to be. At least, not yet.

Another procedure was needed to straighten the remaining half-toe and remove the remaining scar tissue.

I was down to ninety-two pounds, and had absolutely no energy. Most people would've thrown up their hands and given up.

Not me. I was more determined to beat the monster plaguing me.

I prayed multiple times a day. Friends and family prayed for me. Even friends of friends on social media pages whom I never met wished me well, and hoped I made it through without too many emotional and physical scars.

Nevertheless, even with all the prayers, some answered, some not, I believed much of it came from me. I had to do it. I took the extra push and made it work. All of these accomplishments needed to be done, and I had every intention of being the driving force in my move forward.

I had the cheering section, now I had to prove to them I was worthy of their encouragement.

I was blessed.

It wasn't only my determination. I had the best team of loved ones, doctors, nurses, and in-home care on my side. All of them were phenomenal. I couldn't have done it without any of them.

I've had a positive experience with the OOFOS. They helped me recover, and accept my new normal. I was referred to OOFOS from a podiatrist at the wound center who said I'd feel like I was walking on clouds.

Myatt and I set out to find a pair and purchased a pair of OOCloogs. My feet changed and the swelling was reduced. I wanted a pair of OOahh slides. The OOFOS team helped find the correct size.

I must say everyone at OOFOS was magnificent in their willingness to be part of my recovery process.

I don't want to make this sound like a commercial. They deserve the praise and should have the stamp of approval for an excellent job.

This footwear was a blessing and an unexpected bonus to my physical and emotional healing process.

I wore my slides all the time in the house. They're more comfortable than any slipper I've ever owned.

They're awesome. I started wearing them in public. I was extremely self-conscious about my feet and toes. As I progressed forward, I worried less about people noticing I didn't have toes.

I love the way the slides look when I'm wearing shorts and jeans. I use my clogs for work, and with jeans and pants on the weekend.

Walking barefoot, especially if you have issues with your feet, wasn't a good idea. With extensive running or walking, I needed comfortable shoes.

The OOFOS brand helped my recovery.

Mid-April I was walking with my prosthetic comfy, sneakers. Three times a day for about ten minutes each time. We worked hard to get to this point. I looked forward to increasing my endurance and strength.

Even though Emma was a rock of support and encouragement, she wasn't able to look at my feet. When she did, it was a major milestone for her, and a moment of acceptance.

I get it.

I recall one of my aunt's had lost a finger while working at the macaroni factory when she was younger. I was afraid to look at it.

Odd, it was only the tip of her finger missing. As a young child, I saw her damaged finger and thought it was scary.

Since I had no toes, I was curious. Would my children, or other children, be scared of me? Would my grandkids freak out because of my feet?

I certainly didn't want anyone being uncomfortable around me. I've explained to my children it wasn't normal to have missing toes. I understand it was a little freaky.

People do get nervous and make comments.

I've learned not to let it bother me.

It took time. Don't get me wrong. I had to be comfortable with it before I could expect it from anyone else. If I was self-conscious about it, other people certainly were.

I couldn't blame them for their discomfort.

My feet were healing and recovering quite well. I was looking forward to walking around with no socks. There was still a bit of swelling and blisters. I was also having trouble with my left foot rolling on its side. Once that was gone, I'd be in much better shape.

Around this time, I was able to visit Dr. J. He was one in a team of doctors who saved my life, and I developed a kinship with him.

It was almost a year, along with several hurdles, since I saw him. I've kept in touch with him through them all. He continued to inquire about my recovery and healing process.

I'll never forget what Dr. J did for my family and me.

He will always be my hero.

Maria Papalia-Meier

One of the nurses from the wound center recommended a support group and talking with people who went through what I had. It was comforting and reassuring to speak and write to someone who experienced the same thing I had with my feet.

The Amputee Coalition was also a tremendous help. I was able to ask other people who lost their toes for any advice on what they did to prevent their feet from blistering, and if they had any recommendations for shoes.

I had my orthotics redone. Gel was added to the front of the shoes to try and help with the blisters. To increase support, they added orthopedic shoe lifts which helped some but not 100%.

I was also ready to find other shoes I could be fitted with besides sneakers. To me, it was a big step. I was looking forward to different ways to stay active and mobile.

The best thing I was told mid-summer…I could go swimming!

On August 8th, one year after my release from the hospital we had a huge, celebratory party. We rented a water slide and told everyone to bring bathing suits. We wanted to show how much we appreciated their love, help, and unconditional encouragement.

It was a good thing we invited all the neighbors because it was difficult to drive through our neighborhood.

We were thrilled. Almost everyone we invited came to celebrate with us. We even had friends come from out-of-state for the event.

I was excited Joanna and her mother came to celebrate the one year anniversary of coming home. It meant the world to me. With her in North Carolina and us in Massachusetts, it wasn't easy to visit each other as much as we would've liked.

As I was greeting them, out of the corner of my eye, I saw the Lawrence's walk through the doorway. They flew up for the night.

Life was good. I had my two best friends and their families here to help us celebrate.

Love and loyalty trumps everything. Faith, hope, charity…it's all there in one big bundle. But the best of all is the love we've received from family and friends.

The time they spent to help us, the prayers they extended could never be measured. It was as infinite as the stars. Their never-ending support was a priceless gift.

We'll never be able to repay them, or thank them enough.

In December, we celebrated my aunt's one-hundredth birthday! Can you imagine? I loved listening to the stories she told.

This festivity was the first time I took a trip out of Massachusetts since I was sick. I wasn't sure how I would handle it. I was worried about many things.

It was my first traveling experience with my new feet. I wasn't sure if I could cope with my new *norm* outside of the house.

I was out of my element and so far, out of my comfort zone I couldn't see the trees. I had a routine and system which allowed me to get around and manipulate my surroundings.

This was a completely different adventure. I wasn't sure I was prepared.

I was borderline paranoid about catching any kind of germ, illness, or flu. It wouldn't be the best scenario at this point in my life or my recovery.

Everyone who came near me needed to wash their hands. So much so, the children began doing it automatically. Yes, they washed their hands the moment they arrived home from school or an extra-curricular activity before coming to see me.

I didn't eat *community foods*, from buffets, appetizer trays, dessert trays, or plates laid out for munching.

It took years to share foods such as dips, raw veggies, and snacks. I'm getting a little bit better, but am exceptionally cautious.

A salad bar in the restaurant was and still is out of the question. I'd probably get hives if it was suggested.

People touch food, whether intentional or not, and it caused serious anxiety for me.

Kids touch everything…and don't wash their hands properly.

There were too many numerous occasions over the years when I watched someone leave a bathroom stall and not wash their hands before they left the room.

Those type of incidents stuck in my head and refused to let go. The apprehension of not knowing how it happened, or where the strep infection came from was a stick in my side.

My tempestuous fear of not knowing if someone was contagious, or coming down with a random illness, and inadvertently passing the germs onto my family or me fueled my murky borderline paranoid worlds.

It was crippling.

I worried about getting sick, and the nightmare would start all over again.

But with all of these worries, I refused to miss my aunt's one-hundredth birthday party! There was no way.

By the end of 2015, and countless days of physical therapy and downright/outright determination, I was able to practice running.

It would take a while. They gave a detailed routine to follow. The practice, along with a hefty spoonful of strength training and patience, would get me there.

My gait hadn't changed, which was a good thing. With the help of special orthopedic shoes, they prevented my foot from rolling.

There was slight pain and a bit of trouble with my knees, but we'd get past it.

I was on a mission and couldn't wait to run again.

I made a major milestone. Physical therapy was down to once a month. I was encouraged by both doctors and therapists. They repeatedly said the reason for my great recovery was because I was in such good physical shape before the surgeries.

It motivated me to push myself harder.

I *would* be where I was before.

The following months were typical visits to the doctors, and therapists. We concentrated on preventing foot roll, my recovery, and hoped to avoid more surgical treatment.

We made a trip to the Bahamas. According to the doctor, as long as I didn't have any wounds, and prevented my feet from trauma, I could enjoy myself. Of course, being who I am, I made sure they were protected with cast bags.

It was an adventure. I swam with the dolphins.

We had a blast!

Unfortunately, no matter how hard we tried, surgery couldn't be prevented. In October 2016, I went back in for my foot. My half-toe was making my foot roll. It caused extreme pain in my foot and ankle and made it difficult to walk and run.

As part of the procedure, he moved my half-toe over. It helped. The sutures stayed in for three weeks. The pin they put in my toe was there for about six weeks.

Hopefully, this would be the last surgical procedure on my foot.

In a way, I'm glad I waited. When they originally suggested the surgery, I wasn't strong enough.

It was frustrating being in a chair again. My friends and I made plans to go see the Rockettes in New York City. I had every intention of cancelling but they wouldn't hear of it. They didn't care I couldn't walk.

My spectacular group of friends managed to get a wheelchair for the trip and helped keep an eye on Emma.

Chapter Nine

Running was always in the back of my mind.

I enjoyed running and still do. I'm good at it. I run for my health, and for my sanity. It was also an easy way to socialize with others, and find common ground with different people. It was a good conversation starter when you're around a new group and an easy way to connect with people when in a new situation.

Running indoors may be an excellent option for other people. I would rather not run on a treadmill. I prefer being outdoors, surrounded by nature, instead of the loud TVs playing and the consistent noises in a gym. For me running outside is peaceful and quiet. I can hear my inner voice.

After I lost my toes, I was told I'd never run again and needed to find a different sport.

I cried.

It was heart-breaking. I had to deal with the loss. It was dealing with the death of a major part of me. I mourned the death of the old Maria.

It didn't merely hurt physically, but was emotionally devastating. I'm a friendly, out-going person. Not being able to run, wasn't only about no longer being able to run. It was abruptly seizing my means of socializing and networking with people.

It was taking away a part of my soul.

Maria Papalia-Meier

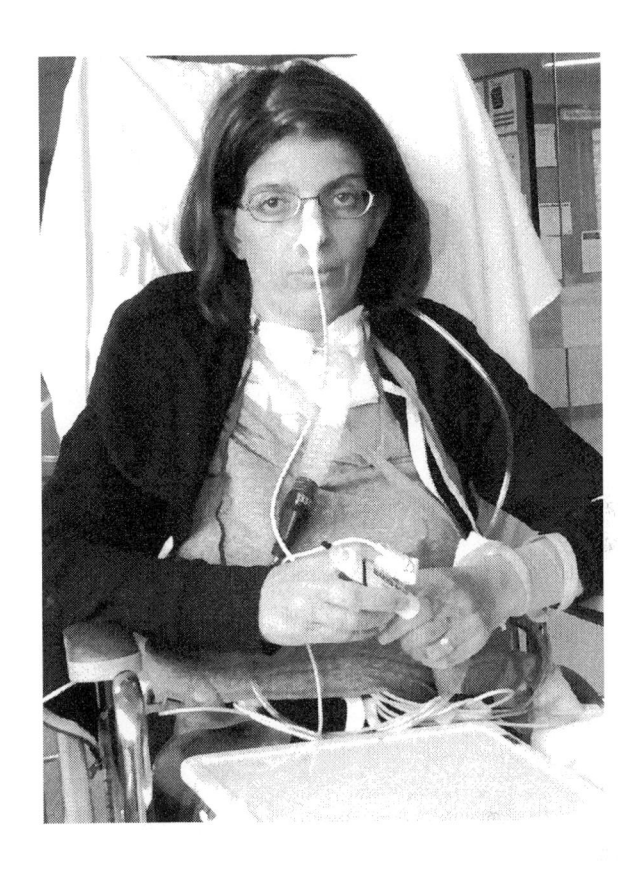

While at Spaulding Cambridge for rehab, they wheeled me outside and I enjoyed the fresh air and weather. I spotted the running clinic sign every time.

It was a constant reminder for me. I would run again, and they would be the people who could help.

I didn't know it'd take over three years, a bunch of ups and downs, and a whole lot of disastrous setbacks. I wanted to run again and the clinic was the place who'd help me do it.

As I went through the multiple surgeries, I was concerned about my health, my weight, and gaining my strength. I did try other things for exercise and entertainment.

One of our friends recommended yoga. Myatt's friend, Russell, started doing it because of issues he had with his back. He practiced yoga on a regular basis. As it turned out, he went from impending surgery to a healthy enough improvement where he no longer needed surgical treatment.

I enjoyed Bikram Yoga, also known as hot yoga. I know I said it before, but I love the heat.

It wasn't exactly something I would've considered. First, I wasn't coordinated. Second, I'm a runner.

At this point, why not?

Janey was a yoga instructor and came to our house for a few private lessons starting with the basics.

What I enjoyed about this form of yoga was its flexibility. There were poses I needed to work with. If I couldn't do the pose completely as I was supposed to, I did what I could. It gave the flexibility to work up to the full poses as progression allows.

As I saw each small accomplishment in the mirror, it was incredible.

Not having toes made it hard to balance. I was amazed at what I accomplished by focusing on each step-by-step set up for the poses.

I enjoyed the challenge.

It was arduous at times trying to do most of the exercises and poses. The moves were centered on creating physical and emotional balance. Without toes, it made it slightly toilsome.

I refused to be discouraged. I would find a way to make it work. If I stayed patient and focused, it would come over time.

I started with a trainer, who helped strengthen my inner core. This led to a better and stronger physical balance needed for any form of yoga.

Yoga helped me focus. The breathing and relaxation techniques helped to reach the peacefulness I needed.

I was a runner. All I ever wanted to do was run. I wasn't interested in doing anything else. Until my life changed and I was forced to adapt to a different lifestyle.

In a way, it was a blessing. It opened my mind to new and different things. If I wasn't amenable to finding other things, I'd never have started enjoying yoga.

It amazed me what the body can do. Once I was able to focus, my balance improved, and I was mentally and physically stronger.

The class was amazing.

I can't do every pose, but I have reached a point in my classes where I can stand on what's supposed to be the tip of my toes. I can balance on one foot and kick the other foot behind me.

I tagged Janey in a post, and a lady in the class commented. She was encouraging and told me I was doing well. She wanted to know how long I was practicing.

I chatted with her briefly and was surprised she didn't know I didn't have any toes. Considering I did the class without socks on, I thought *everyone* in the class noticed.

This sounds a bit silly, or probably narcissistic, but I believe I needed the outside encouragement. At first, I was self-conscious about it, but as time went on, I wanted people to notice. I wanted them to see what I was doing and be impressed.

I wanted to work out again, mainly for my health, and emotional well-being. Exercise helped control my high triglycerides. Those little troublemakers must be kept at a reasonable level. It keeps the numbers down.

If someone asked me to go to the gym to work out, do yoga, or go for a bike ride, I'd go. To be honest, I pushed myself to do it.

Mention running? I'm all in. I couldn't move fast enough to grab my shoes and go! Unfortunately, the option was taken away, ripped from my heart. I still looked forward to the day I could run again.

I'm obviously a stubborn wench. I refused to believe I couldn't run again.

I liked challenges. I thrived on them.

How about ice-skating? I did it. I managed to go ice-skating with my daughter.

And heels? You bet! I took control of my life. I know my body. What it can do and how far I can push it. I am self-aware and have the ability to push or back off when needed. I always had a goal in mind, and refused to allow it to thwart my progress. It may slow me down, but it won't stop me.

Nothing in life was easy.

I worked hard, with tears and personal resolve to reach every square inch of space, and each step forward to get where I am now.

I overcame many challenges and have tripped over many hurdles. But I made it.

I grasped my inner inspiration and punched those obstacles down. They said I wouldn't run. I took their perceived doom, dismissed their declaration of what my limitations would be, and discovered my true potential.

I refused to accept their statistical cynical views. I wasn't going to be one.

What I have told, and will continue to tell people…Never give up. Willpower, from the mind and heart, is the whole shebang. It's what's been and what will be.

I went from being the sickest person to running a half-marathon. I turned my back on the Angel of Death. It wasn't my time. I have fought the reaper, and fought the river of death. I accepted the compelling and intimidating challenges that kept pummeling me in the face.

I merely punched back.

People are the most complex living beings in our world. I was one of those people who always exaggerated how bad I felt.

Never again. I know and understand too much. Like an inexperienced boxer in the ring, I was struck down and knocked out. But I wouldn't let the beast keep me down. I refused to succumb to wallowing in my own tears of woe.

I was no longer the same person I was before my surgeries. I wasn't about to obsess over the negative. Reality was a kicker.

I *was* being realistic.

Toes don't grow back.

I've accepted what has happened. I didn't want to, but honestly, was there another option? I came to terms with what I had to do, and had every intention of controlling what I could in my life.

Here are the brutal facts:

I was in excruciating pain, with what seemed like neverending twists of random setbacks. The beast tried to break me, make me bend in places I never thought I'd go. I refused to die. I wouldn't give in to the weakness of surrender.

I was repulsed by my feebleness.

I shook my fist at my mortality.

I was…

Angry

Terrified

Happy to be alive

And I was loved.

Because of all of those and many more, because of who I was, it only made me stronger. It fastened and deepened the conviction of survival in my heart.

I almost lost my life. It would've been a pretty hefty price to pay for a neglected strep infection.

Who knew such a minor thing could become so fatal?

I revisit those days often and see how much I've gained from all of this. My friends and family were there for me, proving their love and their faith in God.

I am a Runner

I saw life through the eyes of my soul. I had faith — faith of the heart.

I could do anything.

Chapter Ten

After multiple surgeries and physical therapy, I had the grit and resolve to run again. It wasn't going to be easy. A positive and realistic attitude kept me going forward. I wasn't walking around the house with rainbows floating around above my head and bouncing around looking for fairy dust to make my dreams come true.

I knew it was going to be a challenge. I had a healthier more realistic threshold to cross, and I was ready.

Sometimes I think the hope I held onto was much better and stronger when it was done with a positive, realistic attitude. With the combination of hope and realism, I hit the jackpot. It was the perfect balance of affirmation.

I didn't set unreasonable goals. I did it one small step at a time. I made the opportunities real and kept them within my reach. I set achievable targets, and by doing so, I didn't set myself up for failure.

The *doom doctors* said I'd never run again.

I wasn't going to listen to their negativity. I wrapped their *no-nevers* up into a ball of guano and threw them away.

I hired a personal trainer. I picked the hardest, toughest, and most willful trainer available at the YMCA.

He was thorough and perfect for me. We discussed what I expected from him, myself, my ambitions and baseline. I let him know from the onset I wanted to gain my strength back and run again. I gave him full disclosure on my illness and recovery process. I didn't want him to have any surprises.

I saw by his reactions he empathized with the trauma my body went through. He admitted he never worked with someone who experienced what I had, nor done any personal training with someone who had their toes amputated, skin-graphs, and prior ankle stress fractures.

He was enthused and willing to take on the challenge to help reach my goals. I was honest and he understood the obstacles we faced.

He reminded me to be patient with the process and not to hide anything from him. As long as I was upfront with him, I'd be exercising and first-rate again.

The results of my fitness test gave him a place to start. The muscle imbalances affected and hindered my performance. My Overhead Squat assessment into a chair showed him I had no stabilization through the lumbo-pelvic hip complex. (Muscle and connective tissues of the lumbar spine, pelvic girdle, and hip joint.) My legs were unbalanced, my knees adducted and pulled inward, and my upper body, back, and shoulders needed muscular strengthening.

During the fitness test, I managed to do thirteen modified pushups. I was able to plank for twenty-five seconds, which gave him an idea of my lower core strength. He also did a cardio test using a tempo step cadence. After three minutes, he assessed my heart rate over a sixty-second span. I came in at 110 BPM, and my resting heart rate was at 72 BPM.

He was very pleased with the results.

He started with a client stabilization training. We focused on spending extra time on strengthening my ankles and feet.

My first training session was in mid-August. He prepared a thorough program specifically for my physical and emotional needs. As he explained, we worked on my core and balance training. Once it was acceptable, we focused on strength training.

We worked on increasing my endurance with cardio training using rowers and ellipticals. It wasn't running but it got me where I needed to go.

For over a year, I worked my butt off. I developed the strength I needed to run again.

I worked on exercises like planks, marching, bridges, birddogs, stability ball, hamstring curls, and single leg balance, hip raises to help my core, and adduction.

My training continued with adduction cable exercises to help strengthen my ankles, and straight leg kickbacks to tighten my sexy glutes. (Or so I hoped.)

No matter how far I progressed, he always made sure we incorporated balance and stabilization. We used banded stability ball wall squats to improve my squat form, lateral raises, curls, YTIM arm movements to improve my core, back, and shoulders.

Every session and workout had one purpose in mind — to strengthen and activate my muscles to perform at their best.

I was determined.

Modifications had to be made. Imagination and intuitiveness became a standard process. My amputation made basic exercises harder. I was able to keep balanced and upright. My single leg balances were aided with a wall and a cane was used to help with my lunge walks.

With his persistence and my stubbornness, I no longer needed them. I was able to handle more strenuous cardio workouts. I could plank for sixty seconds and perform multiple sets of squats and pushups.

Over the year, my workout time increased and my rest time decreased.

We pushed my limits, and I loved it.

My sites were set on the Spaulding Rehabilitation Hospital's running clinic. I needed to get in the targeted physical shape in order to be accepted at their clinic.

Several phone calls, discussions with the doctors, and consultation appointments were arranged. They needed to consult with my personal physicians and PTs to see if someone could work with me.

I was optimistic about what they could do to help me run again. My doctor needed to approve a prescription for PT appointments. It was through their program where I worked with a specialized physical therapist.

They had to be sure there were no issues, and cleared before they could move forward.

I was honest and explained everything I could, including the surgeries and nerve pain.

I was on their waiting list for months before I managed to get an appointment for an evaluation.

I worried I'd be denied. I worked hard to get to this point in my life. It was a major victory for me to do well on the evaluation, and be accepted to the running clinic.

Once everyone gave me the green light, the clinic had me in for a two-hour assessment. They had me do different balancing exercises, and run on a treadmill — with and without shoes. They videoed the assessment so they could make a thorough evaluation.

When I was accepted to the clinic, it was a huge victory for everyone who helped me. The trainers at the facility taught me the proper way to run, the importance of strength training, and stretching.

There was more to running than simply running.

I'm more aware of my body, how it's supposed to perform, and how to run properly. I appreciate it more, and I don't take it for granted.

My therapist at the running clinic and my personal trainer diligently worked together. The three of us saw the chance for me to reach my objectives.

It was my passion, and I was going to run again!

In order to reach the goal, I did a lot of foot strengthening exercises and core training. I used towel curls, banded plantar, and ankle exercises like dorsiflexion. Of course, they included single leg squats, hops, and side lunges.

I did Kettlebell deadlifts, front squats with dumbbells, dedication to increase cardio, core, balance, and yes, even proper nutrition.

Sheer determination from my therapist at Spaulding Running Clinic, my personal trainer, and my unquenchable thirst for running kept me moving forward.

That's exactly what I did.

Thank the world for health insurance. Without it, where would we be? The people we worked with were kind and understanding. Although, there were times when I had to advocate for myself, most times they were willing to work toward my goal: Getting back to healthy normal life, and being able to run again.

I did a lot of research on my own. It not only gave me firsthand knowledge of what other people were going through, but how to follow through with what I needed.

It was difficult to search information, especially when I didn't know exactly how to word things, what to look for, or where to look.

Going to other doctors or therapists for second opinions was a necessity for me. It may have been for reassurance, or it was searching for the right person who was going to say what I wanted to hear.

Either way, it was a challenge. The more I searched, the more questions I had for my main physician and my orthopedic doctor.

Getting the correct prosthetics was an interesting experience, but I had a lot of help getting what I needed. One of the things I noticed about A Step Ahead Prosthetics was their tag line…*Live Life Without Limitations.*

Challenge accepted.

Retraining, persistence, a positive and realistic can-do attitude with a barrel full of stubbornness, and I was ready to commit to my first race since my struggle with the river of death.

My post-illness racing plans:

The Miles for Migraine run in North Kingston, RI.

The Margarita 5K in Atlanta, GA.

The Zooma Half Marathon in Cape Cod.

I did well with only a few setbacks. I changed my shoes, my running style, and was on my own for several months without any issues.

I participated with others as well as alone. I'm an exceedingly competitive person, and it tends to peak out and challenge those around me. I used to run fast, at least, fast for me. I ran an average eight to nine minute mile.

Running in the heat hadn't worked out well. With the rising temperatures into summer, it wasn't such a great idea. My feet started swelling, and I started getting blisters.

I was not happy.

I threw a pity party for myself. After a few days of wallowing in my pool of doleful tears, I realized it wasn't the way to keep a positive attitude.

Every year on June eighteenth, I take the day off. It's the day for me to do a good deed. I've needed to do it ever since the reaper tapped on my shoulder.

Even though I've helped someone, or brought a smile to a friend in need, I've begun to believe it was more for me. I've told myself it was for others, and reassured myself the good moments were for them.

Being on an emotional roller coaster for the last few years was vexing, not only for myself, but for my family and friends.

I'm no longer sick.

I've struggled with letting go. I've worked on the new me. I don't consider myself 100% better. Many times over the years, I've felt alone and helpless. There was a sense of vulnerability and a need to find what was lost. I wondered where the old Maria was hiding.

There were and are times when I was broodingly morose when I went to work. While I was out on medical leave all of my stations with the exception of one, contacted me via e-mail, text, cards, etc. to check on me and see how well I was progressing. Many of them expressed how much they missed me.

Their lives continued. They had their own personal demands, problems, and issues. Oh, I'm sure they were curious about how I was doing, or checked my Facebook without commenting. The unrealistic sense of abandonment was crushing.

For them, the tragedy of what happened was in the past, and they moved on. They no longer asked how I was doing.

I was destitute, a sick feeling clumped in my belly. I was left behind.

Out of sight out of mind seemed to be the harshest words for me. It was a phrase my husband said on many occasions about different people and different things.

The last time I followed through with my June eighteenth celebration, I visited the doctors and nurses at the hospital.

When I was there, I was told many times, I was the sickest person in the hospital. It wasn't exactly the title I wanted tagged to my name.

When I was staying in the ICU, there were doctors and nurses who called in on their days off to see how I was doing. They were always bright and cheery.

When my mother wheeled me around the hospital areas, they all stopped and said hello, asked how I was doing, and continued to encourage my relentless push to get better. They were glad to see me and were excited about how well I was doing.

They were there for me then. I've wished many times they were there now. Their encouraging words and their friendly smiles and reassurances got me through many days when I wanted to throw up my hands and concede with a shameful, bowed head.

Every day was a battle. It was a constant conflict to stay positive about the girl I was and who I became.

The worst part of recovery was finding, or rather trying to figure out who I am now, and what my purpose was in life. There must be a reason behind why I survived.

Why me?

Why was I the one to get to see the sun shine every day?

So very much changed. I no longer had my successful career I was so proud of doing. I was humbled in a way. My confidence was shaken, and I criticized myself as a wife and mother.

I'm working part-time in customer service. It's an exhausting position. Service reps do *not* get the credit and proper acknowledgment they deserve. I had no indication of how draining it could be.

I'm not handling it well. It's not the company. They're great.

It's a struggle going to work in a less than satisfying job. I go home already worn and exhausted from people yelling at me on the phone.

They know it's not my fault, but it doesn't deter them. They have an ear, who's forced to listen to their rants about not receiving their package or the damage, etc.

The constant complaining wears on a person.

Unfortunately, there are times when my children and husband catch the brunt of my irritation. Some days I'm merely being *that way*.

Don't get me wrong, I'm not above doing this type of work. I had a great job in HR before all of this happened.

I want to do more.

It doesn't fit me. I must acknowledge if the part-time position wasn't available, I couldn't have reached two of my goals.

Running and my SHRM certification. (Society for Human Resource Management)

Who knows where life will lead us? As long as I've raised two well-balance, happy, and productive adults, I'll be satisfied. If I can enjoy life with my fantastic husband by my side, what more could I ask for? I may not have a magical HR career anymore, but I'm surrounded by people who love me.

What I'm supposed to be doing is on its way!

I'm pleased they allowed me to return. Since I was out of work for over a year and a half, they didn't and couldn't hold my position. As a matter of fact, they didn't have to give me a job at all. It was a blessing they did.

They offered a part-time position in customer service, and I took it. I was with the company for over nineteen years. I appreciate everything this company did for me.

It was overwhelming how many people in our community helped, as well. We lived there for such a short time. I had no idea people cared so much.

It was humbling.

Our closest friends continue to support us, and celebrate my little victories. In many situations, I'm fine. In other ways, I'm not. I was unexpectedly severed from who I was.

I'm not depressed.

I can't seem to find the old Maria. I'm uncertain why I'm still searching for her. She's gone. I went through a full-fledged bereavement process. The new me will never be the same. I am a stronger and better person.

Everything comes, everything passes, and everything is replaced.
That's life.

On the last anniversary of my illness, I returned to the place where I struggled within a sunless chrysalis. Brigham Hospital released me from the old chitin and gave me a new life.

It was the spot I would be remembered. It was where they celebrated my victories with me.

As luck would have it when I walked into the ICU, the woman who was my day nurse was there. She was pleased to see us and appreciated the goodies we brought.

She remarked I'd been in her thoughts over the weekend. I was surprised she remembered the date. It wasn't the case. She and her husband went to see Zach Brown and wondered if we attended. It was because of me she started listening to his music.

I was taken off guard. I had no recollection. My husband said he played music on my phone while I was unconscious, and Zach Brown was on the music list.

How funny the little things are!

Chapter Eleven

When times are rough, you rely on your friends and family. I have close friends I've known for a long time.

When we were creating our wedding invitation list, we chose friends we believed we would have forever.

I have heard others speaking about their wedding, who they had in it, and they remarked how they didn't talk to them anymore or hang out with them. They moved on with their lives and gone in separate directions.

I didn't want to be that person.

I do have one regret from my wedding. I wish I asked my dear friend Dianne to be a part of the wedding party. She is and always has been one of the best friends I have ever had.

All of these close friends were by my side when I, and my family, needed them most.

I'll start with my sister. Michelle is a year younger than me. Like most siblings, we had our arguments.

At times, there was a little jealousy on my part. Things came easy for her. She was always the one with good luck on her side. It was obvious she was the favorite.

I called her the golden girl. She had my parent's credit card at school for *emergencies*, which to her meant the sale at one of her favorite stores.

I, on the other hand, worked hard at school, and earned my own extra money.

Several times, we shopped at the mall with my parents at Christmas time and my sister pointed to something she wanted. My mom handed me the credit card, and I bought it for Michelle.

It was irritating.

As I grew older, the resentment and jealousy dissipated. I understood she needed me as much as I needed her.

She was by my side when I was dying. She sat with me and held my hand. She was there for my family the whole time.

We talked about the infamous trip to the hospital. She was at the swimming pool, having fun, and enjoying a peaceful day. She missed the calls from our mom and my husband.

Michelle was shocked when she heard the news. Of course, she had a million questions. Not getting the answers she needed from our mother, she called Myatt.

As soon as she heard I was put on a ventilator, she wanted to leave immediately. Something was severely wrong if I was put on a vent. Myatt told her to hold off until morning. She listened to what he recommended, even though her instinct was to rush to the hospital.

Myatt nor I realized how bad things were. We were under the impression I'd get some IV fluids and sent home.

I've asked my husband about my stats. What was my blood pressure? My pulse? He said I didn't have one. They couldn't get a reading. My temperature? High fever.

I was stunned.

My worst fear was leaving this earth too soon. I wanted my children to know who I was. I wanted them to have great memories of our times together and the fun we shared.

It was a hot, metal rod poking at my heart and soul. I hadn't remembered a lot of things about my father. At my father's wake, I heard stories about him. Stories I wished I'd known. I didn't want it happening to my children.

Sometimes, being frightened is good. It heightens the senses and makes us aware of the crushing storm we're anticipating. I'm not referring to self-inflicted anxiety where I was expecting it all to go wrong. I mean the inherent response to survival and the instinct for self-preservation.

We all have our ways of coping with emergencies and tragedies. Most people go into denial. It's natural to immediately say "no". Our instincts are to avoid problems.

It's human to run away from danger. There are only a handful of brave souls who go toward a fire. People are similar to horses when it comes to perilous situations.

All horses have different personalities, but most equine owners will tell you practically any horse will have a fight or flight moment if they feel threatened.

It's in those moments we have the natural reaction to remove the clutter and survive. Several people I've spoken with have said I talk about this event in my life with emotional detachment.

I probably do. I think it was how I survived. Or perhaps, it was as if it happened to someone else. I'm not sure. It's my way of perceiving the past few years, and separating it from the reality of where I am now.

I'm a bit more philosophical. Time has a different meaning now. I've heard people say tomorrow never comes. I'll take my past and learn from it. I'll enjoy today and swaddle it as the precious gift it is. I'll pray I can have another day with my loved ones.

If I had left this earth, life would've gone on without me. The world would have kept turning. My loved ones would miss me, but as time passed, I'd be a memory. It'd be a sad moment for them because I was gone, and a joyful moment of memories to make them smile.

But it's not going to happen yet. We all leave this earth sooner or later. I've had a second chance to make it a memorable life.

I'm not done. The reaper can stay in his cave. I have so much I want to do, and I have every intention of doing them.

I may never understand or know what my family and friends went through while I was ill and so close to death. For me, I took a nap. I was aware of only a few of the things going on around me.

I have vague memories of getting ready to transfer to Brigham Hospital, the pre-gate nurse, and Joanna asking if I remembered her.

It was two weeks filled with crazy dreams.

I had no desire to face and confront my mortality. I didn't want to pass on to the afterlife yet. There was so much more I wanted to do. A world was waiting for me. One with an abundance of adventures I wanted to experience in life and with my family.

While I was unconscious, I wasn't anxious or fearful.

If I passed away, I may never have known how incredible my friends and family were for me. There's no way I'll ever be able to show or tell them how much I appreciate what they've done. Words will never be able to express the love I feel for them.

They were there when I needed them the most.

I was okay.

Chapter Twelve

The last few years and during the time I was in the hospital, I had plenty of time to think. Multiple questions went through my head.

I asked myself why? What happened? What could I have done differently? What was the catalyst to all of this mess I got myself into? How did I become resistant to antibiotics?

None of it made sense to me.

I believe it happened after our trip to Iowa, perhaps on Father's Day weekend. I wasn't well before that.

Another theory was catching strep while I was in the hospital having my hysterectomy in February. I dismissed the theory because it was several months prior to contracting sepsis in June.

I believe I caught something when we were in Iowa visiting Myatt's family. It was a few weeks after we returned. Years ago, his sister's ex-husband was ill with very similar symptoms. Although we discussed it as an odd coincidence, I dismissed it as a flu virus.

I hadn't contracted strep throat since I was a child. I used to get it often. I understood the symptoms.

I believe my immune system was down. I ran often, and wasn't taking care of myself properly. I was eating the right healthy foods but not eating regularly. I wasn't sleeping well, and I was pretty worn down.

I was working more than usual. I wasn't enjoying it. It wasn't like my job in Atlanta. I didn't want to quit. It was decent money and was hard to give up.

I was stressed.

If I paid closer attention, I'd have realized it was a recipe for disaster.

I was physically and mentally exhausted. I wanted to be done and finished. I didn't want the lifestyle anymore.

I was over it.

In a way, getting sick was a huge wake-up call for me. How's this for taking a tragedy and turning it into rainbows and unicorns? I didn't even know I had it in me.

Oh, yes. Don't get me wrong. I'm stubborn. I'm a type A personality. I'm a perfectionist.

I wasn't aware I had the sort of inner strength needed for something like this.

The brush with death gave me the opportunity to figure out what I wanted in needed in life.

Sometimes, the anxiety will creep in and batter my heart. To know I was in a coma, asleep all that time, it was bizarre. When I awoke, my life fast-forwarded.

I missed a lot in those two weeks!

It's one of the reasons why I decided to share my story. It wasn't only for myself. I wanted to let people know about sepsis and help in any way I could. I needed to write about it for anyone who needed to hear words of encouragement.

My biggest concern is not knowing *how* I became so ill. It's caused a slight germ phobia I've labored against since my hospital stay. It's scary not knowing what or how it happened.

I have intermittent lumps of doom attempting to stagnate and destroy my confidence. I'm anxious. Something was going to happen, and it wouldn't get done. It was a horrible, sinking feeling to believe you've lost time or have run out of time.

The worrisome, déja-vu moments are on a rampage, tapping on my memories more frequently than ever. I want this as a documentation for my family and for anyone it can help.

I don't want any of this experience to be in vain.

I fought the river of death. I emerged stronger than I ever believed I could be.

I fought hard and won.

I asked these questions more times than I can recall. Why me? Why was I the one who made it?

I confess. I had an abundance of survivor guilt when I first arrived home. I'm not joking when I say there's plenty of time to think when lying in a hospital bed.

I pondered everything under the sun.

The *why me*, why did God choose me to live? Why did the beautiful lady next to me in the hospital room pass on to the next world?

Why was I left behind?

Why did her husband and children have to mourn her death while I survived?

I'm not anyone special. I've never accomplished a miracle, or saved multiple lives like the doctors, paramedics, and the heroes of the world.

So why did I survive? I spent years trying to find the answer to this particular question. I'm sure many *survivors* have wondered the same thing. From the Pearl Harbor survivors to the 9/11 survivors, they've all asked themselves that question.

Sharing my experience with this life-threatening event may encourage or help someone reach their goals.

I was chosen as a case study for PT. If I can reach more people, I've done what I've needed to do.

Let me tell you a secret. If you're doing it too, stop. Don't kick yourself. You're not alone.

We returned to Iowa to attend Myatt's niece's wedding. I was twitchy and nervous. I wanted to be there and share in their joyful day, but I was filled with foreboding, and illogical unseen threats.

Such a silly thing, but it triggered memories of my illness and the strenuous efforts to survive the grueling and oppressive struggles to survive.

Apprehension would bear its ugly head whenever I thought about traveling to Iowa. It caused a few heated discussions between Myatt and myself. As much empathy as my husband has had concerning my illness, I don't think he quite gets the numbing terror arising from the aftermath. Just like I can't understand his fear when I was dying in the ICU, he can't quite grasp my reluctance to revisit the traumatic events that brought us here.

When I think about getting sick again, a ferocious beast grabs my chest and squeezes. My heart pounds, my eyes water, and my legs pull me down. I have to sit before I fall.

I've taken anxiety meds. Before leaving for Iowa, as a safety precaution I went to the doctor before we left and had my white blood cell count checked. I wanted to make sure I wasn't ill.

When we were there, I stayed in the house and wouldn't walk around the farm. I washed my hands a million times.

Even though the anxiety was knocking, I had a great time at the wedding.

I didn't get sick, nor did I come down with any infections when we got home. Perhaps next time I'll only need half the anxiety medications.

I don't think I'm prone to colds or flus. My body isn't resistant to antibiotics. I have a hard time accepting it was a freak thing. Because the antibiotics they had me on, I was concerned it might cause future situations with resistance. I was told there shouldn't be an issue.

I've had the flu shot before and won't ever do it again. I don't allow the children to get one either. As far as I'm concerned, the side effects of the flu shots don't outweigh the odds of getting the flu.

Keeping healthy, clean, and avoiding people who are ill is, to me, a much better way of avoiding illnesses.

I am a Runner

Documentation and Letters

Maria's Mother

Septicemia

The day before Maria was hospitalized she called me to say she wasn't well. Thinking it might be the flu, I told her to see the doctor in the morning, and I would be there first thing.

Later in the day, my son-in-law called to say I'd best get there as soon as I could. By his tone, I immediately realized the severity of the situation. I threw some essentials in the car. I was stopped by friends who convinced me I wasn't in any condition to drive the distance.

I also realized I had no idea of what was happening or where Maria was taken.

I'd be complicating the situation.

The following morning I drove to meet my other daughter to go to Boston's Brigham Woman's Hospital to see Maria.

I kept thinking this *is not* happening. I can't lose her.

We arrived at the hospital and called ahead to let them know. I ran for an elevator. I was told I couldn't see Maria until I saw the doctor who'd prepare me for what to expect.

The only words I heard was he'd never seen anyone so affected with ill health in all his years at Brigham.

Surviving would be a miracle.

I sat there thinking I had to wake up from this bad dream and needed to see her. We all stayed at the hospital twenty-four/seven until Maria's condition stabilized somewhat. She was still in a medically induced coma, but her vitals were strong.

I went to be with Carson and Emma who were remarkable throughout this whole ordeal. It wasn't easy on them to be cared for by so many individuals. I hoped my being there would bring some normalcy to their days.

Maria's friends planned Emma's seventh birthday party with friends. One of them brought her a lovely dress to wear.

I couldn't get myself to have her try it on. But one day close to her party, she looked at me and said, "Grandma, I have to try the dress on. I will miss having my mom there because it's not every day a girl turns seven, but I have to make sure it fits."

I didn't find it difficult to allow Myatt to make all the decisions. I was always kept informed and knew it needed to be that way.

Thankfully, the miracle took place!

Every day is a gift. Take nothing for granted. Do not just exist... live.

We only get one chance.

I am a Runner

Maria's Sister

I first learned about Maria being in the hospital by a phone call from my mom. I remembered my girls and I were swimming at our pool and I missed some calls from her and my brother-in-law.

I returned her call. She told me Maria was in the hospital. I was stunned and asked a million questions. My mom was unable to give me any real answers, so I called Myatt. Maria was in the hospital, but he hadn't told my mom she was on a ventilator.

Once he said she was on a vent, I knew something was severely wrong... most of the forty-year-old's I've known don't get admitted to the hospital, and certainly don't get put on ventilators.

It was probably late afternoon by the time I spoke with Myatt. My first reaction was to get in the car! He assured me it was okay to wait until morning. Although I knew better, I went with the plan. I'm not sure my brother-in-law comprehended the severity of the circumstance. He did later when my sister was transported to an alternate hospital for better care.

He told us to come right away.

My brother lives about two hours from the hospital and went immediately. I left first thing in the morning. It was about a four and a half hour drive. In hindsight, I should've gone the second I learned she was on a vent.

I went to my sister's house to meet my mom before going to the hospital. Before arriving at her house, I didn't know what to think. I was scared and so anxious to get there. I'm not sure I had time to process what I was feeling. When I got to Maria's, my mom wasn't there yet. I went inside her garage, and it hit me all at once.

I saw her shoes on the floor and other things. It looked like she was still there, alive and well. I felt her presence.

Without warning, it immediately brought tears to my eyes. I was overwhelmed at the moment thinking, how can this be happening?

I cried for a bit but pulled myself together because I knew my mother would be there soon, and I had to concentrate on getting to see my sister.

When we arrived at the hospital, it was precisely at the right time to be given an update on how she was doing. The resident told us she was the sickest person in the hospital. My heart sank.

It was a huge hospital.

He went on to say her blood pressure was very low, and they were almost maxed out on what they could give her. I think he said more, but honestly, I stopped listening. The situation was grave. All I knew was I needed to see her as quickly as I could.

It may sound crazy, but I always knew she'd be okay.

Our father passed away several years before but something, somehow told me he was taking care of her. I would tell Maria I knew our father was watching us, and we'd talk about what he was saying.

I was desperate to get to her and tell her I talked to Dad, and he promised she'd be okay.

I asked if I could see her alone. I walked into the room and barely recognized her. She was so swollen, eyes closed, and didn't respond to me at all.

I walked right up to her. Put my hand on her forehead and said, "Maria, don't worry. Dad said you're going to be fine."

Telling her directly made me feel calm. I have no idea if she heard me, but, however grim the situation seemed, I never once doubted my father was indeed watching her. She was going to be okay.

What I didn't know was how long of a road we were in for.

Visiting hours were limited in the hospital. The nurses and doctors were incredibly kind to me. They knew I was coming from out-of-town, and they let me stay in the room a lot. I promised I wouldn't get in the way. I wanted to stand by her bed and hold her hand, and massage them and help with the swelling for as long as they let me.

The majority of my time was spent at the hospital. I often slept there and gave my brother-in-law the chance to go home and be with the kids. I did spend one night at my sister's house, and I slept with Emma.

I knew they were scared and tried to comfort them as much as I could. I wanted them to return to New Jersey with me, to give Myatt a break and to help offer some distraction. Myatt didn't want them to leave because he wanted them home as soon as Maria woke up. I understood and left the invitation open-ended if he changed his mind.

I did spend a lot of time with Myatt. The first thing I thought was…wow, this man really does love my sister. It made me feel good. He handled things as well as he could. I got to know him a lot better. It was hard for me to have someone else responsible for making decisions for my sister.

I work in healthcare and definitely have my own opinion. Sometimes we bumped horns. Most often though, we were there for each other. He called me every day I wasn't there to let me know what was going on.

I appreciated him keeping me in the loop with how she was. Sometimes, he sent me a video or picture, the first time she moved her hand and another when she moved her foot. I found myself watching them over and over because I was beyond excited to see life come back to her! It took my breath away. It was like watching your children take their first steps!

I felt horrible. I couldn't be there all the time. I had two girls at the time who needed me. It was a hard juggle.

Sometimes I feel bad I don't know the struggles and lasting effects of what happened to her. For example, losing her toes. To me, seeing how far she has come and how sick she was; it was minor. Then, I remember it isn't minor, especially to her. I regret not acknowledging it.

The experience changed my life forever in many ways. I realized in an instant the only thing that really mattered was the health of those we love. Everything else was stuff.

The other thing I learned was how final life is. It can change in one second, which people always say but don't realize until it does.

I never doubted my sister would be okay. I remember telling the doctors we'd care for her no matter what her condition.

This was my sister and what happens to her happens to me.

I thank God every day without exception for letting us keep her. Without her, I would be less than whole.

She gave me a necklace I will never take off. It reminds me of the strength of love and prayer. It has helped me have faith in hard times in my life.

It was a long road for her, and I am so proud of her. She has come so far.

Dianne

My Pap…

I will never forget the emotions I had when Myatt called me about Maria.

I pulled into the parking lot of the kickball fields, getting ready for a fun evening when my phone rang. When I answered Myatt calmly said Maria was in ICU in the hospital, I replied, "Shut up!"

Well, you see…my best friend in life, Maria Papalia (AKA Pap), was always a bit of a hypochondriac. For instance, she was concerned something would happen to her when she swallowed toothpaste. Myatt and I have given Maria a hard time about always being sick, or thinking she was going to die.

Myatt and I have the same sarcastic sense of humor Maria loves!

After my initial reaction, Myatt said she was in the hospital. I could hear in his voice he was trying to be strong and hold himself together, but he was crying. I asked what was wrong, and he let me know Maria had an infection but had no details to pass on yet.

I hung up the phone and cried my eyes out. My heart was physically in pain. My Pap was in ICU, and I wasn't there.

I called my Mom and just cried. All I knew was Pap was in ICU, and Myatt was with her. I didn't know where Carson and Emma were. I wasn't sure if Sandy, Michelle, or Johnny was called. I didn't know much, simply because I was in shock and hadn't ask Myatt anything except how was Pap.

Once I pulled myself together, I got out of the car and found my husband. I let him know what was happening. I remember sitting on the bleachers seeing the kickball game, but my mind wasn't there.

I was nauseous. My hands shook while I tried to text my prayer warriors asking for everyone to begin to pray for my Pap.

I knew I needed to go to Maria. The thought of her in the hospital without me there was horrifying. To be honest, I'm not sure what I thought I was going to do or what difference I was going to make, but I knew I wasn't staying in Atlanta while Pap was in a Boston hospital.

After the kickball game, we immediately made arrangements for me to fly to Boston the next day. I knew my husband would handle our boys while I was gone.

I called my boss and let him know I wasn't sure what the situation was, but I wouldn't be back to work. I needed to go to Boston.

I remember walking through the Atlanta airport crying. I cried through security, sitting at the gate, on the plane, getting the rental car, driving to the hospital, and walking into the hospital.

I headed into the ladies room to pull myself together before I saw Myatt.

By the time I arrived at the hospital, Sandy, Michelle, and Johnny were all there. Myatt met me in the hall, and gave me a brief update. We walked to the ICU waiting room to see her family before we went to see Maria.

He warned me Maria didn't look like herself, and was bloated due to all the fluids she'd been given.

As I followed Myatt back to ICU where Maria was located, I remember thinking, *oh God…Oh God…Oh God…*

I am *not* a fan of hospitals…as a matter of fact, I am scared of hospitals.

The ICU consisted of the Nurse Triage in the center and the patient beds encompassed it. The patients' areas were separated by curtains. As Myatt and I approached Maria's bed, I didn't see Pap. You see, *my* Pap is petite with natural curly hair, and always with a beautiful, healthy tan. The person lying in bed was swollen and pale, with a green tint to her skin.

The sight of her lying in the hospital bed surrounded by nurses and having tubes, wires, cords and a trach was overwhelming. This was something I would never *un-see*.

There was a nurse at Maria's head and a nurse on both sides of her. There was one nurse whose only purpose was to monitor the ECMO machine and document it.

The other nurses were watching all the machines and discussing their observations. There were three or four nurses assigned to Maria twenty-four/seven.

It confirmed the seriousness of the situation.

As I stood on Maria's left side and touched her arm, Myatt was near her feet and lightly touched her leg.

With all the nurses, machines, tubes and wires there wasn't enough space to stand. There wasn't much on Maria's body we could touch without moving something important.

I remember a piece of paper taped to the curtain by her right foot. It had several items listed. Myatt explained the items were what needed to be monitored. Maria had to reach each goal.

At this point, Myatt was with her for twenty-four hours. He was well-versed on each of the goals and the meaning behind them.

He touched Maria's legs and told her she was doing well, and he loved her.

For the first twenty-four hours Myatt, Michelle, Johnny, and I took turns spending time with Maria. Whoever wasn't with her tried to sleep or rest as we waited in the ICU Family Room.

As far as I know, Sandy didn't go back to see Maria. Her heart was broken. Her baby girl was fighting for her life. As a mom, I cannot begin to understand the fear Sandy had in her heart.

Sandy told us, "I just want to hear Maria say *Ma*."

Hearing it broke my heart.

Myatt and I were sitting next to each other talking quietly. Myatt's heart was broken and filled with worry.

We talked about how Maria handled the kids, scheduled birthday parties, and the day-to-day stuff. Maria and he would go back and forth about doing the dishes after dinner, and how ridiculous the disagreement was in the scheme of things.

I dreaded saying goodbye to Maria, but I had to go home. I hugged everyone goodbye, and prayed for them all on my way down in the elevator.

I remember crying quietly as I left the hospital, drove to the airport, walked to my gate, and flew home. Once I got home, I burst into tears and sobbed.

I was scared for Maria, Myatt, Carson, Emma, Sandy, Michelle, and Johnny.

Over the next week, I spoke to and texted Myatt and Michelle several times each day to get an update. I prayed for her all day, every day.

At one point, I remember fighting with the copier at work and asking God to help me get this machine to work.

It hit me.

My Pap was fighting for her life and here I was arguing with the copy machine. The thought stuck with me. It made me really put things into perspective.

We had our summer vacation planned to visit Aruba. I struggled with going or staying home. I remember thinking Aruba was one of Maria's favorite places on earth.

I knew she wouldn't want me to miss out on visiting Aruba, but in my heart, I was struggling. I was leaving my friend and going to *her* favorite place.

Myatt was kind enough to encourage me to go. He would text updates while I was in Aruba.

We visited Maria's favorite church, Alto Vista Chapel. We walked the Stations of the Cross and ended at the chapel. We knelt and said a prayer for Maria and her family.

We prayed for all the doctors and nurses who were in Maria's path.

That particular day, there was a family outside the church selling items they made by hand. I bought myself and Maria matching beaded crosses. I took a few pictures of us at her favorite place and knew I'd share them with her once she was back to normal.

I flew back to Boston to see her again after we returned from vacation. I remember placing the cross I brought her on the pillow close to her head. She was still unconscious, but the nurses were expecting to bring her out of the coma very soon.

They mentioned Maria would be confused and may be aggressive if she didn't see someone she knew while she was waking up.

Her leg near her knee was damaged and peeling. I also remember seeing her feet. They weren't completely black yet, but they looked unhealthy.

Myatt explained about her body's natural instinct to save her organs, and the proper amount of blood wasn't going to her extremities. It didn't occur to me she stood a good chance of losing her toes.

Her fingers were discolored and peeling, but they weren't near as bad as her feet and right leg.

Myatt continued to update me over the next several days and weeks. I returned to visit Maria when she was moved to the rehabilitation hospital.

She still had the trach and feeding tube. She was also having dialysis. She was dead set on having the trach removed. She had to pass the swallow test.

The nurses conducted the swallow test while I was there. I remember watching Maria as she tried so hard to pass the test. She continued to get choked up on the mucus in the trach.

She was so upset she didn't pass the test. She couldn't understand why she couldn't have ice. It broke my heart to see the disappointment and then the anger of not being allowed to have ice.

I was able to spend a couple of days with Maria in the rehabilitation hospital. We would talk about her fears and concerns, as well as the normal miniscule day-to-day activities of life.

We watched TV and I read my book while she rested. Maria and I had some interesting conversation during this visit. She was convinced her current employer, FedEx, and UGA, the Georgia Bulldog Mascot were in the news.

She had her laptop and was Googling stories about FedEx and UGA. Needless to say, she couldn't find anything on the Internet. But we certainly did talk about it for a while.

The other thing she was laser focused on was buying a large house in Tennessee or North Carolina and both of our families moving in together.

While it sounded like a lot of fun, it was impossible. Needless to say, I agreed with her, and we searched the Internet for homes where all eight of us could live comfortably.

Maria had insisted Myatt not come visit her one evening after work. Looking back, I understand she wanted Myatt to have a little more time with the kids while I was there, and he didn't have to worry about her.

I tried to talk her into allowing him to stop by if he chose. She was adamant.

Guess who got to make *that* phone call?

Me!

I could hear in Myatt's voice he was disappointed, and genuinely worried about his wife. I'm sure he felt better once he saw Maria and her progress each day.

Maria kept saying her feet hurt. I mentioned it to the nurses but not a lot could be done to help.

I asked the nurse if there was something I could do. She recommended an ointment I could rub on Maria's feet.

I offered to do it. The nurse went over a few things with me and gave me gloves. Maria's toes were black, and I had never seen anything like it before.

I put on the rubber gloves and got to work. I rubbed the ointment on her feet and toes. I was careful not to pull or rub any loose skin off her feet.

The nurse had explained the lose skin needed to come off naturally. I remember rubbing her feet as she relaxed. It was one thing that would calm her nerves.

Understandably, Maria was anxious while she was in rehab. She simply wanted to go home. She kept trying to convince me she would be fine at home.

I would mention she couldn't go home because she wasn't strong enough to walk yet.

"How would you get to the bathroom?"

Pap responded, "Crawl."

I wanted to laugh out loud. But honestly, she saw crawling as a viable solution to the problem.

Joanna

Maria,

I'm not surprised you're writing a book about your experience. I've been so proud and inspired by how you handled everything since getting out of the hospital. Maybe I don't know all of your worries and concerns, but you've always stayed so positive and optimistic while going through the many surgeries. Now you and Myatt are both running together and getting yourself back to where you want to be. It was hard work, and probably slow going at times, but you're doing it — living life to its fullest!

Your sister, Michelle, called to tell me when you were in the hospital. I remember I was leaving the grocery store parking lot. I also remember it didn't seem real — like I was hearing the story of someone else other than you. Then I remember thinking, wow, she's in the ICU, and Michelle said you were one of the sickest people in the hospital.

But I still wanted to be skeptical. Maria's strong and healthy. It's not her time. Her kids still have so much more time with her.

Driving home, I started thinking what if this really is it? What if I don't see her again? The news took time to sink in for me to really process the seriousness of it all. The only thing I could do was wait for updates and see when you were allowed more visitors.

Arriving at the hospital, I didn't know what to expect. A million thoughts ran through my head, like what if she doesn't recognize me? What if something happened and now she's worse?

I remember feeling like garbage because we went to a concert the night before, and I was hung over. I kept thinking, my poor friend was so close to death, and I'm out at a concert and getting drunk! I felt guilty for having fun...

At the hospital, I knew you had to be getting better since they were allowing more visitors. When I saw your mom in the waiting room she said you were much better, but to still prepare myself. After all, you were still in ICU but stable.

Your mom was so concerned when she told me they almost lost you. The nurses also told me you were hooked up to a lot of machines and you may not be responsive, and you really couldn't talk yet (because of the tubes). But you could shake your head, etc. So then, my nerves were really getting to me before I went in.

I remember walking in and seeing you lying there. My heart sank and my throat felt tight. I wanted to cry but stayed strong so you didn't feel bad. I wanted to tell you I loved you, even if I didn't call as often as I should.

All the old memories came flooding back. It was really emotional. When I saw what had happened with your feet and circulation, all I could think was she'll probably never be able to run again after this. She'd been so into running, and it'll be taken away.

So of course, I was deeply affected after seeing you go through this experience. It reinforced how we cannot take our health for granted. Strong friendships will never fade, no matter how much time passes between visits.

The biggest change was I stopped feeling bad for myself having RA. And wouldn't limit myself about what I could and couldn't do. I was only doing gentle yoga at the time, and thought I was active enough in my day-to-day house and yard work.

Your love of running made me curious if I could get back into it. I hadn't run for exercise since college. So I started going to the park after dropping the kids off at school. I ran a mile, then worked up to two, three, four — I really could do it — and it felt great!

I ran my first 5K in September of 2016 and started getting us into family mud runs. Our family was always into the outdoors, but now we're trying new events and activities. The best was doing The Great Race with you for the first time last year.

It meant so much to me. You were getting stronger and we did a race like that considering where you were three years earlier.

Health has become our focus. We're eating better and are down to two or three drinks per week. (Only on weekends.) You've changed me in positive ways that will last a lifetime. Now, if I could fit in more sleep!

Stay strong!

Your friendship means the world to me.

Celeste

I forget which day of the week it was, but one day I arrived at the house like I did every day to get the kids off the bus. Maria's car was in the driveway. I thought it was unusual but brushed it off.

When I got Emma and Carson off the bus, they told me Maria had stayed home from work because she was sick. I didn't think much of it because they told me she had a cold. The next day when I arrived Maria's car was still in the driveway.

Shortly after, Myatt texted me and told me he had taken Maria to the doctor, and they had to go to the hospital. I wasn't aware of how severe the situation was.

Myatt asked me to tell the kids they'd be able to see them off the next day. I still wasn't aware of how sick Maria was. I informed the kids she had to stay at the hospital overnight so she could get better. They'd be able to see her tomorrow after school. They were worried and sad. I made sure to comfort them. She was okay, and they would see her super soon.

It was crazy!

There was so much going on every day. I tried my hardest to make everything as normal as possible for Carson and Emma. For the most part, it was the three of us at the house every day with family leaving and coming here and there.

Along with family, there were so many friends. Friends would check in with me daily to see if there was anything we needed, anything they could do, and ask what was going on.

We kept busy with activities, homework, and playing with friends.

The children expressed worry and concern every day. This was hard for me, because I wasn't always sure what was going on.

The second day was the hardest. They had it set in their minds they'd be able to go see their mom at the hospital after they got home from school.

Myatt informed me it wouldn't be possible. Breaking this news to them wasn't easy. They didn't understand why. They were super excited and had asked as soon as they got off the bus.

When we got into the house I casually said, *hey you're not going to be able to see Mom today but hopefully soon.* Of course, there were tears, lots of them, especially from Emma. As time went on, they always asked lots of questions and had lots of tears.

Bedtime was the toughest. Every night we talked about how tomorrow was a new day, and we were one day closer to seeing Mom.

The neighbors and friends were so great. So supportive, kind, and willing to help with anything. The first night Maria wasn't home Emma asked me if she could give me a kiss on the cheek since her mom wasn't home to give her one.

So cute!

This situation definitely changed my life. I'm grateful I was able to be there for Carson, Emma, and the whole family. It was stressful, but I wouldn't change anything. My love for Carson and Emma grew immensely. The whole Meier family will always be a part of my life.

I will never forget this time.

I am a Runner

Leigh Ann

Dear Maria,

When you told me you were thinking about writing a book about your experience the first thing I thought was this project would be the perfect thing for you. Not only does your story show how quickly life can change, but also how it is possible to persevere and come back stronger after a life-altering event. Yours is the story of how with the positive attitude and strong commitment to your goals, it's possible to achieve with may seem impossible.

When you have asked me questions about the weeks leading up to your illness, I can't remember much. Maybe because it was unbelievable, you had become so sick in such a short period of time, or maybe because things became hectic so quickly I may have blocked it out.

I was so scared for you and your family. Once it was clear you were going to be okay, I put those memories away for good. When I see you now, it actually seems like none of this ever happened.

I'll do my best to recall everything and hopefully this will help you with your project.

We were running together for quite a long time before you became sick. The last long run we did was supposed to be an eight-mile run the Saturday before Father's Day. We headed down to the center of North Attleboro as this was our route for longer runs.

We turned around sooner than planned. I don't think it was your idea to turn around because I remember struggling with the run as well. We decided about three miles in to turnaround and head home. I think we ran about six miles.

Later in the day, I talked to you while you were pulling weeds around your mailbox. We were debating on whether to run the next day, which was Father's Day. In the end, we decided to take the day off and run again on Monday.

That Saturday afternoon you had showed me the rash on your arm. Since you were doing yard work, I thought it was a reaction to something outside. You mentioned it was also on your stomach, which I did think was strange. I believed it was allergy related. You didn't seem worried about it, so I didn't think any more of it.

The next time I saw you was for our Monday morning run. We met outside at 5 a.m., our usual time. I remember you said you felt feverish and might be coming down with something.

You still wanted to run so we set off for our usual three-mile weekday run at our usual pace. This one went normal for about the first two miles, then all of a sudden you stopped and asked me to hold Bash's leash while you fixed your hair.

It was definitely out of character for you. You seemed a little off so we walked the remaining mile back home. I asked if you were still going to work. You said you'd take some Advil or Tylenol and still go in.

A few hours later, I saw your car back at home. I texted to see if you were all right. You responded you were feeling a little worse so you came home to rest. Your text didn't really sound alarming, and I thought you had come down with a regular flu or cold bug and needed a little rest.

Over the next day or two, I texted you to see if you had felt any better or if you wanted to run. Your replies were very short and vague.

No, still sick.

Then one day, I think it was Thursday, Myatt called and said he was taking you to the doctor. The sitter was getting Carson and Emma, but she needed to leave at six p.m. He wanted to know if your kids could come to my house if you were still gone. It wasn't a problem, so when you didn't come home, she brought the kids over at six.

I am a Runner

She returned to get the kids and take them back to your house. I asked if she had any news, and she said you had strep throat and pneumonia. But again, it seemed bad, but not something to cause alarm.

A little after five a.m. the next morning, my phone rang. It was our neighbor. She sounded very alarmed and asked if you were okay. She was on Facebook and saw a strange post from Myatt, and you weren't answering your phone.

I opened Facebook and saw the post. I realized you were very sick, but I still didn't know exactly what was going on.

I called another friend, and she didn't know anything either. We met outside. After all the kids left for school, we tried to decide what we needed to do.

We decided we'd each try to get ahold of Myatt. When either of us heard anything, we'd update each other.

A few hours later, we ended up talking to him. That was when we got the news you had gone septic and how bad the situation really was.

I was so shocked. I didn't believe you could get so terribly sick so fast. We found out your mom, sister, and brother were either already there or on their way.

It became very hard to get ahold of Myatt so we stalked your house. As soon as anyone arrived, we ran over to get any news they might have. As the weeks passed, it was how we received updates.

We wanted to go see you in the hospital. You were in ICU and visitors were restricted. Once you were moved out of ICU, we knew we could come see you.

Whenever we asked Myatt or your mom when it would be a good time, they seemed to talk us out of it or said you weren't up for visitors.

Finally, one day we heard Myatt needed to be at Carson's baseball game, and your mom and sister had gone back to their homes.

We were sure you were all alone.

We decided to surprise you, even though we were pretty sure you probably preferred to know we were coming. We were beginning to think if we let anyone know we were going they'd try to talk us out of it.

Unfortunately, things came up, and it looked like we wouldn't be able to make it after all. We decided to try again another day. But then, one by one all of our obstacles fell away.

Our husbands arrived home early from work and grilled our dinners in record time. The kids' activities either got canceled or the dads could take them.

We left immediately.

We had no idea where we were going but somehow we drove straight to Spaulding Rehab Center and found your room with no problem at all. We laughed about it later because the rest of our trips to the center weren't so easy.

One time we got locked in the parking garage across the street from Brigham.

It was clear to us we were meant to go see you, at exactly that time.

When we walked into your room, I was alarmed at the scene in which we found you. You were almost falling off the bed. I mean, one little bump and you would have landed on the floor.

We lifted you back onto the bed, and we noticed you weighed almost nothing. You were so weak you couldn't even pick up your phone. When you talked, it was only a whisper.

Even though Myatt had explained all of this to us, it was still alarming to see you this way. We also noticed the sheets were in need of changing, so she headed off to find fresh sheets so we could at least clean you up.

You didn't seem surprised to see us. Maybe Myatt had told you how persistent we were, and you were expecting us to show up announced? At any rate, it seemed like you were glad we were there, because you had a ton of questions for us.

You didn't remember much of the weeks prior to when you fell ill. We answered as much as we could. You had a lot of jumbled memories you wanted us to help figure out. You asked us many questions about signs of your illness and behavior.

You had also asked about Carson and Emma and how they were handling the situation. We assured you they were fine. Although for the most part, they were unaware of how sick you were.

While we were there, someone had come into the room to reinsert your feeding tube. I felt horrible watching you go through everything, and seeing you with it made me realize how far you still had to go in order to be well enough to come home.

For me, the most inspiring part of your story starts after you came home. It wasn't immediately apparent you'd lose your toes. Watching as you struggled with the realization you'd have them amputated, and dealing with the grief of what you'd lose…fighting to overcome what others would call a disability was what was truly inspiring about your story.

I can't even begin to count all the times you said various doctors and specialists warned you'd never run again. Each time you became more resolved. You'd keep seeing more doctors until you found one who would help you.

Even if it required more surgeries and physical therapy, you never gave up or lost hope. I never once heard you say you'd hang up your running shoes.

Many times, it seemed you were back on track to resuming your usual running routine, only to have your feet or ankles start to hurt again.

You'd be back to square one.

All of those setbacks led you to the people who would eventually help you. I have no doubt this book you're writing will inspire others to continue to fight for their goals, even if the medical community says it's impossible.

I've told many people about your story, and they are always amazed. I'm so blessed to have you in my life, and very grateful to call you my friend.

I wish you all the best of luck as you start this new endeavor as I know it will provide a positive healing tool which will hopefully allow you to put some closure to this period of your life.

You will do amazing things, my friend. I'm sure a new chapter is starting for you.

I am a Runner

Nancee

I first learned about Maria's hospitalization on Wednesday, around four in the afternoon. The kids were home from school. My husband had also just gotten home after going to an early Red Sox game. I remember hearing his phone ringing.

"If you're asking me if this was my wife, I'd transfer her to Brigham's Woman's Hospital. Yes, I think Maria needs to be somewhere else." He hung up and explained to me what was going on.

Maria was in Norwood Hospital. They think she had pneumonia and had her intubated.

Being a medical professional, I knew it didn't sound right. Maria was an otherwise healthy woman. If Norwood felt the need to intubate, she was seriously ill.

Both of us work at Boston Hospitals. Call us hospital snobs. We don't know of anything bad that's happened at Norwood, it's simply we believe the best care for the sickest is in Boston.

We went on with our evening, dinner, homework, and getting the kids to bed.

I couldn't stop thinking about Maria.

What was going on? How could she be this sick so quickly?

We went to bed early. I was awake when my husband's phone started receiving text messages from Myatt. I started texting him and answering the text, first letting him know it was me.

Myatt had asked about how to get her transferred to Brigham Woman's Hospital. He wanted to know if we knew anyone who could help.

My husband worked in the dialysis department, not inpatient. I texted a friend of ours who worked in the towers and asked for advice. She didn't have much to offer. I know I told Myatt he had the right to get Maria transferred, and he needed to be persistent.

Early the next morning, I contacted Myatt and found out she was transferred to Brigham. The only other thing I remember from the text was Myatt telling me she was on ECMO.

My heart sank. She was gravely ill. Having worked in pediatric cardiology for ten years, experience told me ECMO was a last ditch effort to keep someone alive.

I was scared for her, terrified for Carson, Emma, and Myatt.

How could she be so close to dying?

I was able to see her on Thursday morning. Luckily, my job has a bridge connecting me to Brigham, and I was able to walk over.

I remember looking at her, but it looked nothing like her.

She was puffy, hooked up to so many machines, and infusions. It was difficult to explain, but it was like I knew it was her, but at the same time, I was waiting and telling myself it couldn't be her. I tried wrapping my head around it and wondered how it was possible.

Myatt looked so strong and helpless at the same time. He was on autopilot. He was taking it all in and holding it all together.

It was easy for me to digest the information. I understood the medical jargon and knew the battle her body was up against. I understood it was under attack and the medicines they were pumping into her were to save her life. All the lifesaving medication could also cause damage.

Myatt seemed to understand how critically ill she was. I was hoping he wouldn't ask me too many questions. I didn't want to be dishonest but at the same time, I didn't want him to know how afraid I was for her.

The next time I stopped by, Maria's mother and sister were there. The doctors told them to take it hour by hour. It was clear her family understood how ill she was. They were focused on staying positive.

I was amazed. In these situations, it's necessary to stay optimistic, grasp onto hope, and support each other.

I was thankful Myatt felt comfortable letting us into the situation. When feeling helpless like we did, it was nice to know we could at least explain things or listen to Myatt and know what he was talking about. It's difficult to explain what was going on to some non-medical people. I remember letting them all know if there were any questions, needed anything, we would be there.

I visited her many times. I specifically remember seeing her and her fingers were black. I don't think people would believe it. The body is an amazing thing. It was able to recover.

When I visited her at Spaulding, she was in a wheelchair, and had an NG tube. She looked so thin. Her voice was raspy due to the trach.

We were there visiting when she found out she had to go back into the hospital. She was devastated.

It was a step backward.

Maria Papalia-Meier

Spaulding Hospital's Documentation

The patient was presented to Brigham and Women's Hospital with strep toxic shock syndrome and subsequently developed hypoxemic respiratory failure and septic shock acute kidney injury, and hyperbilirubinemia waiting for recovery from septic shock. She was discharged with the diagnosis and septic shock status post antibiotic therapy with multiple antibiotics, toxic shock syndrome, and respiratory failure who presented on trach trial with trach-mask, and ventilator.

The patient developed toxic shock upon presentation to the intensive care unit with lactate of 7.1. She became hypoxic, and arrested in the intensive care unit on 6/19/2014. EKG showed ST myocardial infarction. The patient regained pulse after chest compression. TTE on 6/19/2014 showed an ejection fraction of 15 to 20%. Repeating TTE on 6/20/2014 showed slightly improved to LVEF up 20 to 25% on global hypokinemia. No wall motion abnormality.

During hospitalization, infectious disease was following the case due to complexity. She was treated with clindamycin, vancomycin, ceftriaxone, and zosyn. Eventually antibiotics was completed. She has not received any antibiotics since 7/1/2014. She did present volume overloaded. She developed hypoxemic respiratory failure likely due to ARDS related to strep toxic shock. The patient was on ECMO from 6/19/2014 to 6/27/2014 and was weaned off from AC to PFC. Trach collar had been placed. She was continued on ventilator and on trach mask trials.

Maria presented with hyperbilirubinemia which increase direct bilirubin from admission. Total bilirubin was 1.6 on 6/19/2014 to max total bilirubin 51.8 on 6/27/2014. RUK ultrasound negative for E/O cholecystitis and hyperbilirubinemia was felt to be due to biliary stasis/acalculous cholecystitis. She presented with fever after ECA mode continuation. Fever likely with unclear etiology. Differential included antibiotics, line-related infection versus pneumonitis. Culture was negative. She did not receive antibiotics and remained hemodynamically stable since.

During hospitalization, she presented with AKI due to ATN due to shock and anuric until 7/9/2014. She was successfully transitioned from CVVH to intermittent hemodialysis several days prior to discharge. During all hemodialysis, right IJ line was placed at 7/3/2014. On 7/9/2014, the patient had five hundred milliliters of urine in her bladder which was straight cathetered with negative cultures.

She was noted to have presenting bleeding aborted trach placement attempts several days prior to discharge and s/o was still bleeding. After that event, she was bronchoscoped with removal of several blood clots. She had right-sided pulmonary failure and infiltrate noted on several chest x-rays around that time which was felt to be due to the bleeding more likely than infectious.

She was noted to present extremity hyperperfusion in the setting of hypertension and pressor supported. The patient's extremities essentially her toes became ischemic and dusky. Vascular was consulted following case as an outpatient. Presently with keeping site clean with Xenaderm twice a day.

During hospitalization, she presented with mental status changes follow back episodes of anxiety. She is presently on Seroquel.

Assessment and Plan:

Respiratory failure on ventilator, acute respiratory distress syndrome, likely due to strep toxic shock. The patient will remain on ventilator.

Pulmonary and respiratory consult placed. Follow case closely ordered. Chest x-ray ordered to follow up shortness of breath and patient on trial for stopping vent. Sputum culture sent and arterial blood gases.

Status post septic shock. What follow-up labs and cultures. Urinalysis and culture and sensitivity bordered. Blood cultures will be ordered over the weekend. CBC ordered. She stopped antibiotics and been off since July 1, 2014.

Left knee ischemic necrosis/skin, necrosis/hypoperfusion.

Care ordered per recommendation of vascular surgery. Plastic and podiatry will follow up case here during hospitalization.

Anxiety. She is on Seroquel p.r.n.

Acute kidney injury on hemodialysis. Comprehensive metabolic profile has been ordered. Follow-up with renal.

Dysphagia. Speech language pathology consult requested. Remained nothing by mouth. Feeding tube and Nepro forty milliliters per hour continued.

Code status. She is a full code.

Follow-up at Brigham and Women's Hospital with doctor from vascular surgery with appointment. Follow-up of necrosis of toes and also necrosis of shin of left leg/knee.

Sepsis

Sepsis is a potentially life-threatening condition of the body's severe response to an infection. If it progresses to septic shock, it could lead to death.

An extreme inflammatory response of the body may be caused by any type of bacterial or viral infection, such as pneumonia or influenza. It can also be caused by parasitic or fungal infections. Sepsis is subtle and can mimic flu and virus symptoms.

When sepsis occurs, the immune system goes into overdrive and begins to attack the body, causing damage to multiple organ systems. It's considered severe when it causes organ failure.

If there is a considerable drop in blood pressure, it's called septic shock. It bears the highest risk of death and complications.

Sepsis is a medical emergency and must be treated quickly and properly for survival.

Do not self-diagnose. Always consult a physician, and when in doubt, make an appointment or go to the emergency clinic.

It's important to look for the warning signs of sepsis. Spotting these symptoms early could prevent the body from septic shock and could save a life.

S – Shiver, fever, or very cold

E – Extreme pain or general discomfort ("worst ever")

P – Pale or discolored skin

S – Sleepy, difficult to rouse, confused

I – "I feel like I might die:"

S – Short of breath

    Sepsis Alliance commissions annual polls to get a better idea of how many people know about sepsis. At the time of this writing, the most recent poll, done in mid-2017, showed there was progress in awareness, 58% of adults in the U.S. have heard of sepsis.
    Unfortunately, many don't understand what it means.
    Listen to your body, and be aware of what it's telling you.

Images

Warning:

The following pages contain images which can be considered graphic in nature, disturbing, offensive, and may not be suitable for some readers. Images may cause discomfort or trigger unpleasant memories.

Images are not intended to cause fear or discomfort and are strictly being used to report, enlighten, and educate readers to the dangers of sepsis.

Discretion is strongly advised.

Maria Papalia-Meier

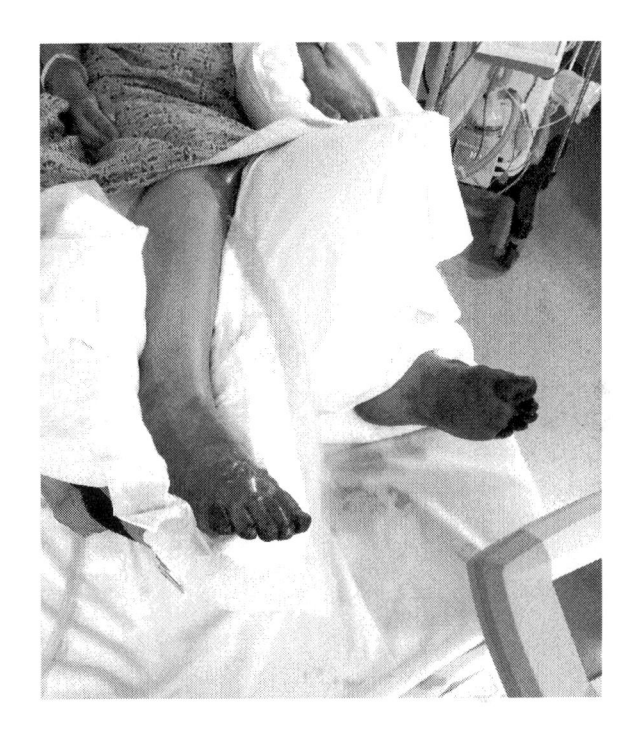

I am a Runner

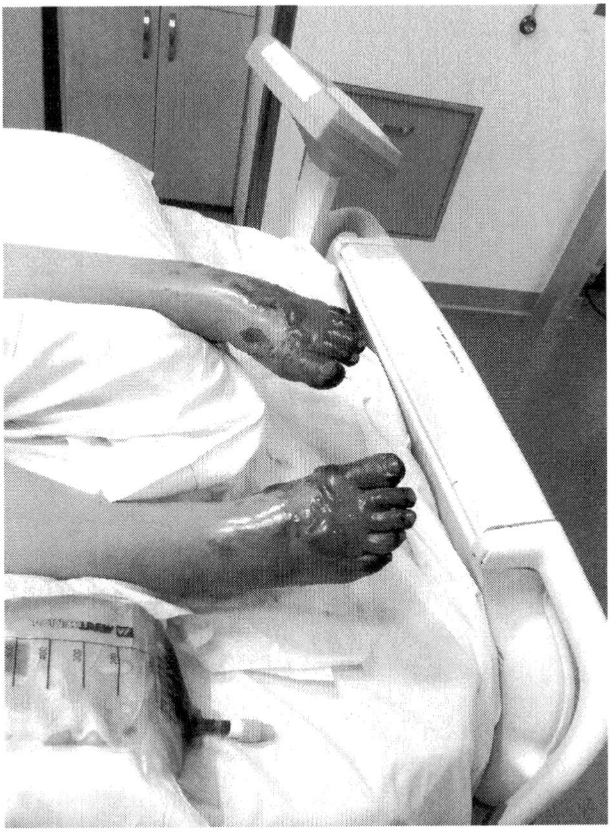

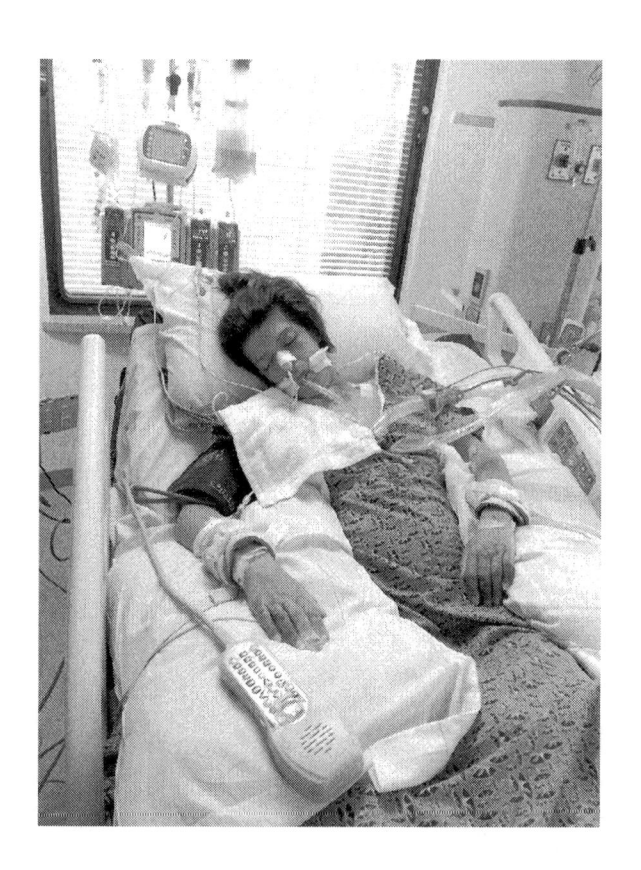

I am a Runner

Maria Papalia-Meier

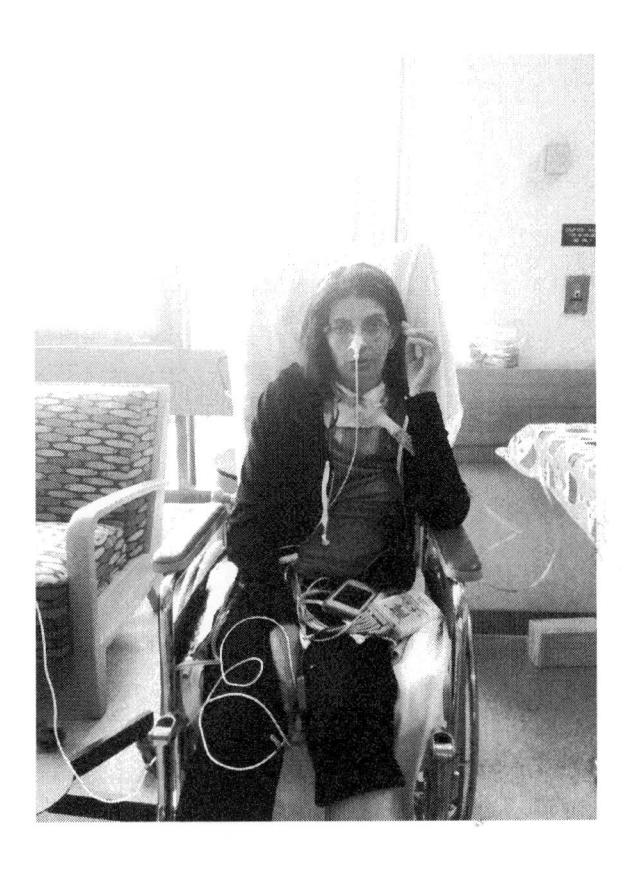

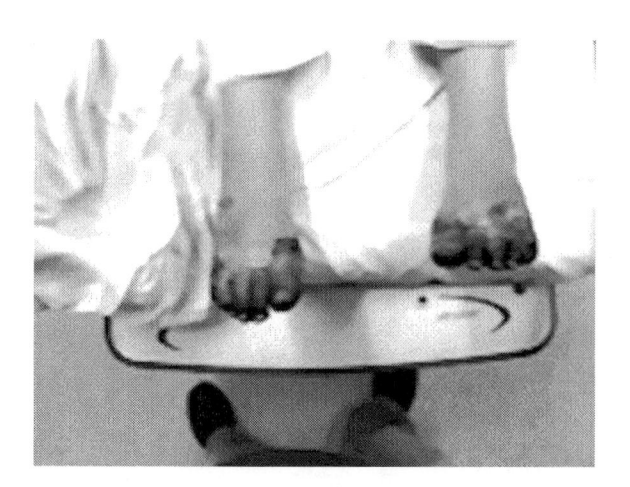

I am a Runner

Maria Papalia-Meier

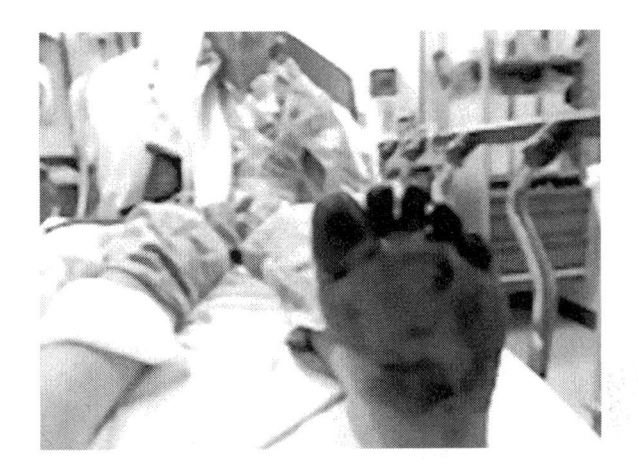

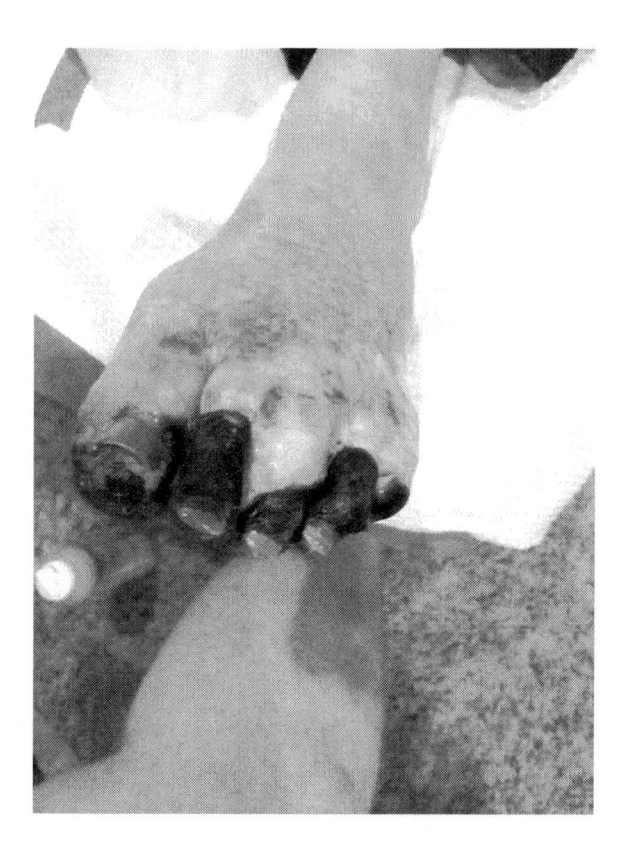

I am a Runner

Maria Papalia-Meier

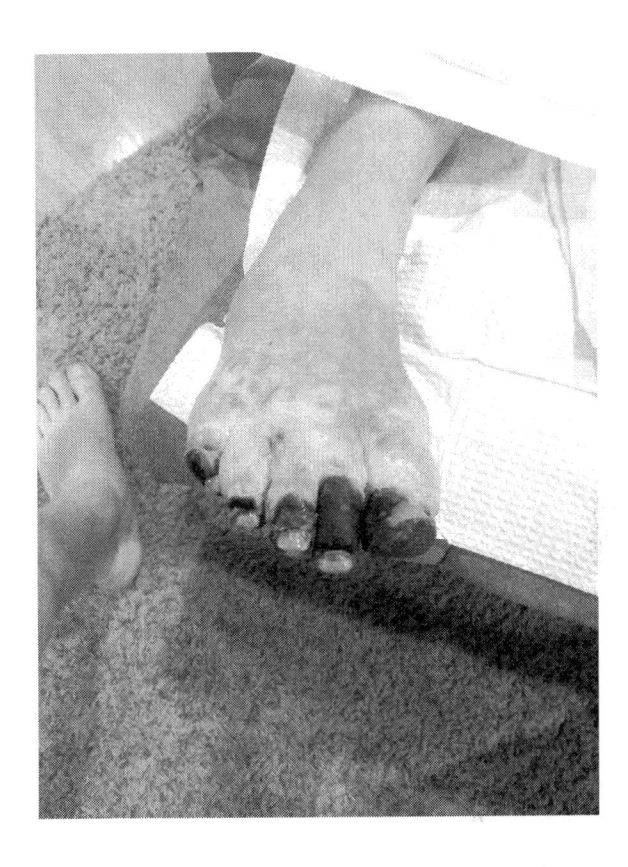

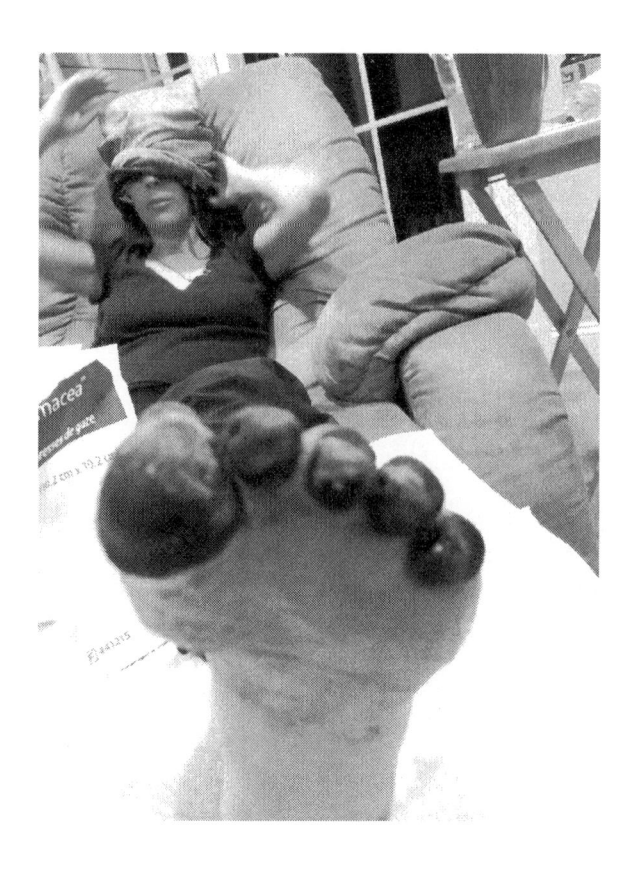

I am a Runner

Maria Papalia-Meier

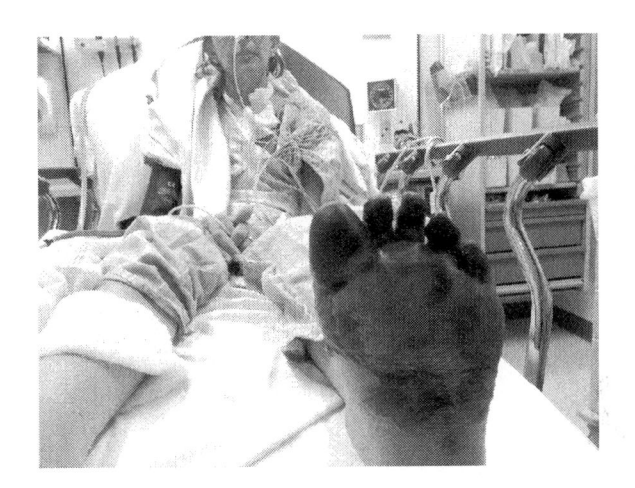

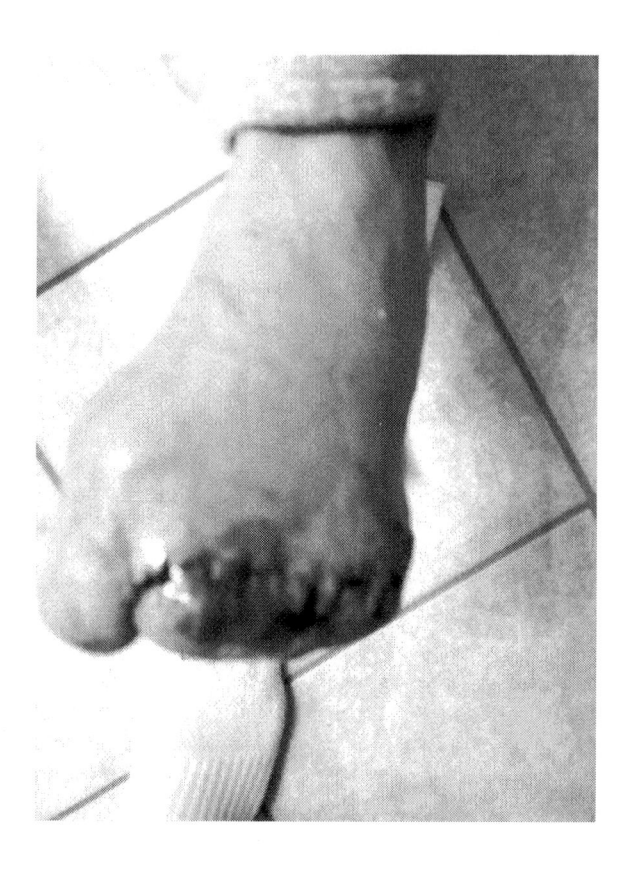

I am a Runner

Maria Papalia-Meier

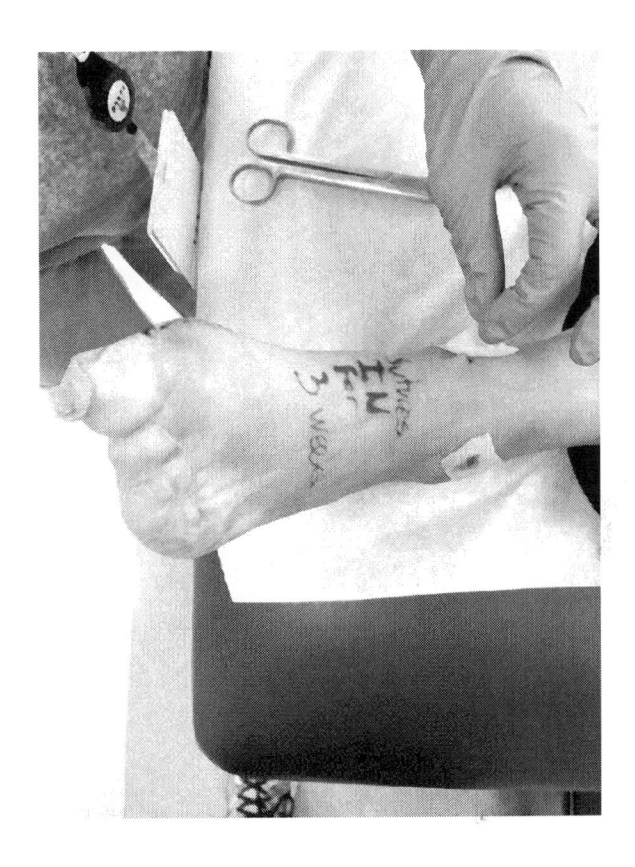

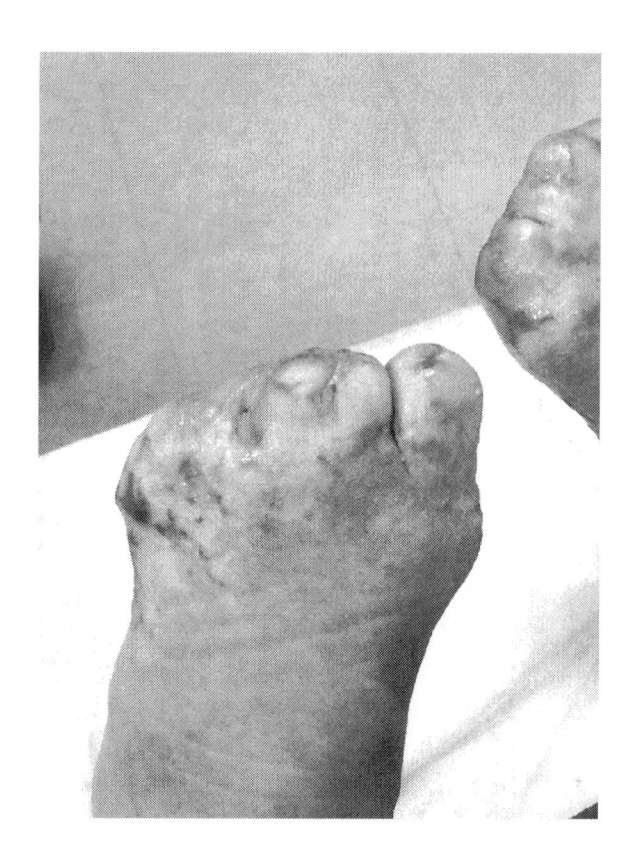

I am a Runner

Maria Papalia-Meier

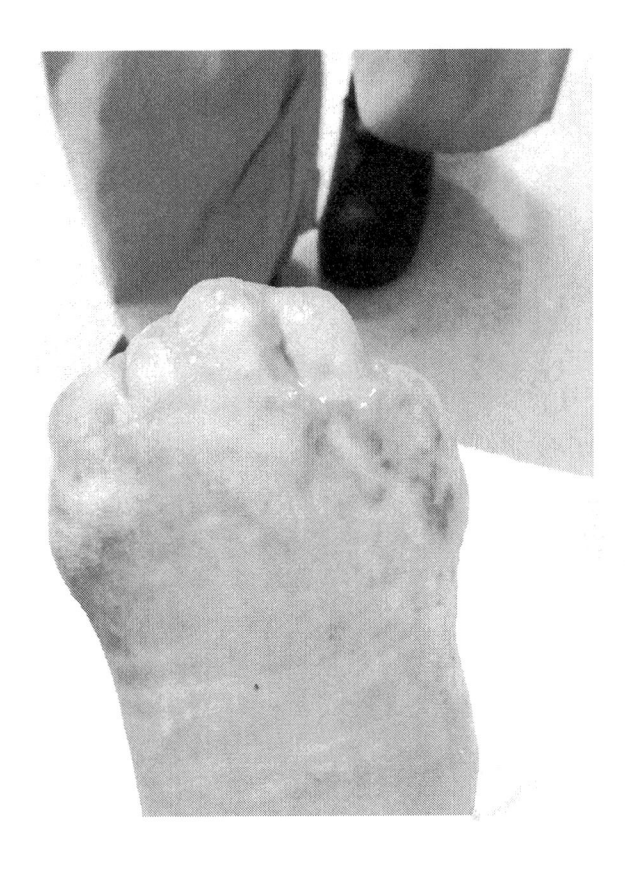

I am a runner.

And I ran again…

Informational Links

Sepsis Alliance — Sepsis.org
Mayo Clinic — MayoClinic.org/diseases-conditions/sepsis/symptoms
Sepsis CDC — CDC.gov/sepsis
Sepsis — WebMD.com/a-to-z-guides/ss/slideshow-sepsis-101
Septicemia — WebMD.com/a-to-z-guides/sepsis-septicemia-blood-infection

Made in the USA
Middletown, DE
04 July 2019